D0859537

Teach My Kid—
I Dare You!

The Educator's Essential Guide to Parent Involvement

**Sherrel Bergmann,
Judith Allen Brough
David Shepard**

EYE ON EDUCATION
6 DEPOT WAY WEST, SUITE 106
LARCHMONT, NY 10538
(914) 833–0551
(914) 833–0761 fax
www.eyeoneducation.com

Copyright © 2008 Eye On Education, Inc.
All Rights Reserved.

For information about permission to reproduce selections from this book, write: Eye On Education, Permissions Dept., Suite 106, 6 Depot Way West, Larchmont, NY 10538.

Library of Congress Cataloging-in-Publication Data

Bergmann, Sherrel.
Teach my kid, I dare you! : the educator's essential guide to parent involvement / by Sherrel Bergmann, Judy Brough, David Shepard.
        p. cm.
    Includes bibliographical references and index.
ISBN-13: 978-1-59667-085-3
ISBN-10: 1-59667-085-1
1. Education—Parent participation. 2. Parent-teacher relationships. I.
Brough, Judith Allen. II. Shepard, David, 1950- III. Title.
LB1048.5.B468 2008
371.19′2—dc22

                                        2008007668

10 9 8 7 6 5 4 3 2

Also Available from EYE ON EDUCATION

Teach Me – I Dare You
Brough, Bergmann, and Holt

Lead Me – I Dare You:
Managing Resistance to School Change
Sherrel Bergmann and Judith Allen Brough

Dealing With Difficult Parents
and With Parents in Difficult Situations
Todd Whitaker and Douglas Fiore

Family Reading Night
Hutchins, Greenfeld, and Epstein

Family Math Night:
Math Standards in Action
Jennifer Taylor-Cox

Family Math Night:
Middle School Math Standards in Action
Jennifer Taylor-Cox and Christine Oberdorf

The Administrator's Guide
to School-Community Relations
George E. Pawlas

Classroom Motivation from A to Z:
How to Engage Your Students in Learning
Barbara R. Blackburn

Classroom Instruction from A to Z:
How to Promote Student Learning
Barbara R. Blackburn

Differentiated Assessment
for Middle and High School Classrooms
Deborah Blaz

Handbook on Differentiated Instruction
for Middle and High Schools
Sheryn Spencer Northey

Dedication

This book is dedicated to our parents, who motivated and supported us throughout our schooling: Betty and Harry Pearsall, Julia Allen, Rose and Jack Shepard.

Table of Contents

Introduction

Why a Parent Involvement Program Design Is Necessary

Does the following sound familiar?

They appeared to be quite normal as they entered the school office early Monday morning—mid-forties, nicely dressed, and polite to the secretary as they asked to see the principal. They knew they should have made an appointment, but they would wait until the principal could see them. They were

   A. Parents of a troubled youth

   B. Parents who had an issue with something being taught in a literature book

   C. Parents who wanted their child transferred to another teacher

   D. Parents who were anticipating a move to the district

   E. Parents who were afraid their son would be getting a B in chemistry

   F. Guardians of a student who was being honored for achievement

   G. Parents of a student who had been kicked off of the bus for fighting

   H. Parents who had missed the high school orientation meeting

   I. Textbook salespeople

Though all of the above could be true, they were actually a set of parents frustrated that their adolescent had been doing so poorly academically since he had entered the ninth grade. Because they had had so little communication from their child, they decided one morning to go to the school and see what was causing this rapid decline. They were concerned and confused because their son had been a high achiever in middle school, an athlete, and highly motivated to go to college. Within two months, he was failing three subjects, had a new set of friends, refused to join any teams, and stopped communicating with his parents. When asked why he was failing, he replied that those dumb teachers at the high school did not know how to teach. All they did was talk all day, and they were boring. They did not accept late assignments, had too many tests, and did not explain things so that he could understand. The parents felt lost. How could there be such a drastic change in just a short period of time? Because their son could not remember his counselor's name, they decided to go to the only person they knew, the principal—who was already late for the mandatory Monday morning administrative council meeting in another building.

The Principal's Response

The principal was

- A. Happy to see parents who cared about their child
- B. Worried about missing the meeting in another building
- C. Concerned about the student
- D. Sure that the student was right about some of the teachers
- E. Unaware of the student's problem
- F. Sure that this would take more than one unannounced meeting
- G. Thinking that this was a bad way to start a week
- H. Making a phone call to the counselor

Again, though all of the above could be true, the reality is that the principal had a personal set of goals that listed students and parents first. The administrative meeting would have to wait. The problem and concern would be dealt with now. But this problem was all too common in the school. Freshmen transfers were having a harder time than usual transitioning to the high school. More and more parents were appearing in the principal's office with a new attitude.

As home communication between parent and student decreased, the number of students who were having serious problems in school increased. As the parents grew frustrated with the many changes that they saw in their child, they assumed that all of those changes were the result of what was going on at school.

These same parents had observed many changes in their child during elementary school as well, but they had been at the school for numerous activities and events. Their child wanted them to be room parents, chaperones, and volunteers. They knew their child's teacher and could communicate daily if necessary. If their child was having a problem of any kind, the teacher usually called them for assistance. They felt needed and capable of helping. The elementary school was in their neighborhood, which added to their feeling of confidence.

When their child entered the middle school, that child became a member of a team of teachers and had an advisor who communicated with them. Teams sent home newsletters and regular progress reports. There were notes from teachers about good work and missing work.

Students gradually tried to be more independent, but the school kept the parents informed. Even if the school was exceptionally large, the teams made it seem smaller and more personal to the parents. Although their young adolescents did not want them to be as visible, they still needed and sought their parental support. They were connected to the school and felt comfortable going there. Although the parents were not as involved in actual classroom activities, they knew the expectations and could monitor their child's progress at home. Through school Web sites, they could even monitor their child's progress on a daily basis. There were homework hotlines to check on the latest assignments. With the transition to the high school came a new parental attitude that was a reflection of their lack of communication with their child.

They came to the principal's office, explained their frustration with their adolescent, and said, "We need some help."

Deciding to Take Action:
10 Steps for Designing a Parent Involvement Program

This book is about how schools can take that dare and involve parents in all levels of their child's learning. Too often, parent involvement issues are reactive rather than proactive. Issues evolve because the school has not established a comprehensive program for involving all parents. The 10-step model requires a commitment of time and resources in a school. If the goal is to increase the quantity and quality of parent involvement, then this model can be useful. Each of the steps in the model is elaborated in the following chapters of this book.

Step 1: Appoint a design task force for parent involvement. This task force should include at least two parents from each level of a K–12 school district or two parents from each grade level of a middle or high school committee. There should also be administrators, teachers from several grade levels, and students. Art, music, physical education, and special education teachers have unique insights and should also be included in the task force. This task force should meet at least three times a year to ensure program continuity.

Step 2: Write and agree on the roles of school personnel (see Chapter 2). The task force should set a timeline for its work and select a leader, recorder, and public relations coordinator. The job of the public relations coordinator is to ensure that accurate work from the task force is being publicized in all school communications to parents.

Step 3: Determine the current level of parent involvement in the school. The task force should decide what demographic data would be useful to them in designing a program (see Chapter 1) by obtaining the following information:

- Current research on parent involvement: Who is involved, when, where, why, and how?
- Interviews with parents of graduates and current students about how they were and would like to be involved
- Interviews and surveys of students about their perceptions and needs
- Interviews with staff members about how they currently involve parents in their classes

Step 4: Set process goals for the task force.

- What will be the parameters of their work?
- What is their timeline for each component of their work?
- What will the final program look like?
- How will technology be used in parent involvement?

Sample goals: To increase the percentage of parents who are involved with individual teachers by 30 percent, or to assess parents' understanding of the curriculum requirements needed to advance to the next level of schooling (elementary to middle to high school and high school to college).

Step 5: Divide the work into action groups for each goal and get started. There may be a demographic data gathering action group. There might be a group that looks at what other schools of similar size are doing. There might be a group that reviews current materials that are sent home, or a group that looks at how parents are informed of student progress. The action groups will depend on the goals, but the work should be divided to move the process along. (See the Resources section at the end of this book.)

Step 6: Complete the data gathering phase and analyze the data. Parents' needs are determined by the data, and goals are set to meet those needs. Data should be analyzed by both grade level and school level. The needs of parents in elementary school are far different from those of high school parents.

Step 7: Design materials and activities to meet the needs of the parents and the goals set by the task force (see Chapters 3–6). For example, a template for increasing the amount of contact between teachers and parents follows:

> Based on data that has been analyzed by the task force, our school will help schools and parents work together by doing the following activity:

> Beginning September 7, all school staff will make one positive phone call per day to a parent regarding the successful work of a student. Administration and counselors will be included. Staff will call a different parent each day. Staff will document the time, date, student's name, phone number called, and whom they talked to on a contact form that will be turned in to the school secretary each Friday afternoon. She will maintain a master list of contacts and submit monthly reports to the faculty.

Step 8: Present the program overview to the staff and parents of each school for input and approval. Then offer teacher training in conferencing strategies and other parent involvement techniques.

Step 9: Recommend strategies for parent roles in crisis intervention (see Chapter 6).

Step 10: Gather data on parent involvement in a systematic way so that the program can be evaluated and changed as necessary.

Variables That May Affect the Design Process

As the school designs and implements the model, there may be variables that affect the process. Some of these the school can control, whereas others are the product of where the school is located.

- ◆ It does make a difference how old the children are.
- ◆ It does make a difference how large the school is and how geographically connected parents are to the school.
- ◆ It does make a difference how much mobility there is in the community and how long students stay in a school.
- ◆ It does make a difference how and when connections to parents are made.

- It does make a difference whether teachers accept their roles and the goals of the model.
- It does make a difference whether students understand the purposes of parent involvement, especially at the middle and high school levels.

There are many barriers to effective communication with parents, with a second language being a major problem for teachers. But none of that will change unless the school designs a comprehensive program to get parents involved early on and keep them involved throughout their child's entire education. The roles of parents are constantly changing because their child is constantly changing in his or her response to the school. The authors of this book bring the point of view of an administrator, a counselor, and a teacher to this process. They have interviewed successful schools, students, parents, and teachers to gain the perspectives offered. They have faced almost every type of parent imaginable and offer profiles of some of the most challenging and the most helpful.

The bottom line is that when parents are positively involved in the schooling of their child or adolescent, that child or adolescent does better in school.

1

Who Makes the Dare? The Myths and Realities of Today's Parents

Program Design Task:
Identifying the Parents in Your School

During my first year as a high school sophomore English teacher, in late October, a new student was brought to my class. He had been kept out of school since age eight by a father who needed his help in the logging business that he owned. The boy had minimal reading and math skills and certainly was not ready for high school English.

The principal told me to do whatever I could to bring the boy along and to help him catch up. The father had always assumed that the boy was incapable of learning and was angry that the truant officer had discovered the boy at home. Being new and ready to help any student, I approached the father, who was still in the school office, and asked whether there were any books at home for reading practice. The father looked at me as if I was crazy and asked me whether I was one of the teachers who was going to teach his son. When I replied "yes," he snickered and said, "Teach my kid—I dare you."

Almost every teacher has a story about a parent whom he or she has encountered. Most parents have had some schooling. Teachers know their kids and their subject areas. Most would agree that parents' attitudes toward and values regarding schools have changed.

Forty years ago, the teacher was one of the most respected professionals in the community. Parents told their children that teachers were always right. Parents visited the school when invited and attended concerts and classroom events. They rarely questioned the school or its teachers. If a student was in trouble in school, he or she was probably in even more trouble when the parents found out. But as the world began to change, parents developed new expectations.

Twenty years ago, when parents were asked, "What would you like the school to provide for your child?" the overwhelming response was, "When my child goes to school, more than anything else, I want to know that he or she is safe." The second most popular response was, "I want to know that when my child is in school, he or she knows at least one adult well enough to go to if support is needed." Other responses from this landmark study (Garvin, 1987) included,

- I want to know that the school is concerned about helping my youngster develop constructive friends.
- I expect that the school will provide my youngster with opportunities to get involved in activities.
- When my youngster comes home from school, I want to know that he or she has had enough good experiences to want to return the next day.
- While my children are in school, I want to know that the school is teaching them what they will need to be prepared for the next level.
- While my youngster is in school, I want teachers to keep me informed of his or her progress.
- When I visit the school, I want to feel welcome by teachers and administrators.
- I'd like to know that the school is making every effort to provide opportunities for parents to be informed about what to expect from youngsters over these years.

Fast forward to the current time frame, and parents' expectations are not much different. The administrators and teachers whom we have interviewed tell us that parents today are asking,

- How do I know that my child is safe in school?
- When can I visit the school?

- What should my child be able to do in reading, math, and other subjects?
- What will schools do to help my child fit in?
- What will the school do if my child is behind academically?
- What options do I have to choose a different school?
- What are the learning standards for each grade?
- What are the safety and discipline standards for the school?
- How can I get involved with the school?
- Who will be my child's advocate in the school?

The concerns and questions have not changed much in 20 years, and parents are still the most powerful ally that a school can have in helping a child learn. The parents of today, however, are more vocal and apt to dare the school to teach their child. With charter schools, homeschooling, school choice, and alternative schools available, parents and students have more choices in the learning environment and often think of changing schools before trying to become involved in the current school. New federal laws require that schools prepare programs for parent involvement. As parents and their expectations change, schools need to respond to all the dares that are made.

Gathering demographic data is easier than arriving at an accurate perception of parent expectations. There is a broad range of parent expectations—from those who expect the school to meet every one of their child's needs to those who just want the school to teach their child to read and write and do math. Parents' expectations are often reflected in students' attitudes toward school, particular subjects, and specific teachers. Teachers' expectations of students are often based on a family's history in the school. Too often, second-generation discrimination occurs when a teacher believes that a student will or will not succeed because of the actions of an older brother or sister.

Teachers make assumptions based on the information they are given. Their time with parents is actually quite minimal. Parents often have several teachers to get to know, while teachers probably see only one student from a family at a time.

As a school designs a program for parent involvement, educators must first ask several basic questions about their clients:

- Who are our parents, and what do they need from us in order to help their children be successful in school?
- How do our parents compare with typical parents today?
- What is typical in our community?

- How many parents are working?
- How many are single parents?
- What percentage of parents graduated from high school themselves?
- How many parents are encouraging their children to stay in school?
- What do parents expect from teachers? How do we know what their expectations are?
- How do they communicate with each other?
- How have parents been involved in the past?
- What are their perceptions of what we do in the school?

Once these questions have been answered and analyzed, a task force for parent involvement can be convened to write a program that is specific to each school. Task force members should include teachers, parents, counselors, administrators, and students. Roles and goals must be written and agreed upon. Demographic questions about parents can be answered with surveys, interviews, student enrollment cards, and census data. The task force should analyze the data and then proceed with program development.

With so many definitions of family and parenting circulating today, teachers must know how to separate myth from fact when planning to involve parents. As teachers and administrators make efforts to meet and greet parents and guardians during the traditional open house, they only know what they see and what parents tell them. Often, parents' needs are not known to the school. Each of the case studies that follow chronicles actual parents functioning with children and adolescents who are in school right now. They illustrate the myths and realities that schools live with every day.

Case Study #1

A 31-year-old single mother is a high school dropout, has a 13-year-old middle school daughter, and boys who are nine and six. She also has two ex-husbands, a job as a bartender in the evening, and the goal of giving her kids an easier life than she has. She rarely makes it to school events and is always working during conferences. She wants her kids to succeed in school, but she has to contend with

- Lack of child support
- Lack of control over her work schedule
- Lack of personal knowledge about the school curriculum

- Lack of money for up-to-date technology in her home
- Information from two different schools

Her daughter is a straight-A student with dreams of going to medical school someday. Her sons do well in school, although one is having some early problems with reading.

Myth

Economic income and marital status do not affect parent involvement in schools.

Reality

"Parents of students living in a household above the poverty level are more likely to be involved in school activities than parents of children living in a household at or below the poverty line" (Child Trends Databank, 2003). According to census data from 2005, there are more than 20,000,000 children living with single parents today. Most of those live with a single mother (U.S. Census Bureau, 2005).

During an evening middle school parent information meeting about the upcoming outdoor education program, the principal asked parents what they need from the school to be able to participate more and become more involved. A parent said, "Please ask how many of us are single parents." When the principal asked, more than half the group raised their hands. A productive discussion followed, and the outcome was a single-parent support group that would meet at the school once a month, would be facilitated by the school counselor, would offer babysitting, and would help them help one another with their students. They formed a phone network to check on out-of-school activities that their young adolescents were asking to participate in. Out of a simple question at a meeting came some ways to help parents and students that the school had not anticipated.

Case Study #2

They are 45-year-old professionals who have two high school sons and a daughter in middle school. They travel to seven countries on business during the course of the school year and are frequently gone at the same time. There is a grandparent who stays with the kids when the parents are out of town. They are very interested in getting their adolescents into an Ivy League school and call teachers whenever it is convenient for them. One of their sons is enrolled in honors classes, and one has a learning disability that requires special tutoring three times a week in school. Their daughter gets good grades, but she is starting to skip classes and hang out with some newfound friends who do not like school.

They have to contend with

- ◆ Busy work schedules that often take precedence over their family time
- ◆ Schools that would like them to be involved with their children, but limited time to do so
- ◆ Lack of information because the kids do not want them to know what is going on in school
- ◆ Lack of information about their kids' friends
- ◆ Secondhand information passed from the school through the grandparent

Myth

As a group, today's parents want the same things from schools that parents have always wanted.

Reality

As a collective group, these parents are called Gen-Xers. They were born between 1961 and 1981 and have very specific goals for their schools and their children. As students themselves, the Gen-Xers are more aware than were their predecessors, the baby boomers, of what is going on, how institutions work, how to manage social relations, how to cope with adults, and how to get things done (Strauss, 2005). Today, they make up most of the elementary and middle school parents and a rising share of high school parents. They account for more than half of all K–12 teachers. They will continue to exert their influence at all school levels through parent organizations, legal issues, and as individuals. They assume that they have easy and direct access to teachers and expect accountability in everything from grading to safety. They are more interested in local than national issues and want proven and cost-effective solutions to problems. When they volunteer at school, they focus on their own child rather than the group (Strauss, 2005). They want schools to make their lives easier rather than harder, to use technology as they use it in the workplace, and to market directly to them. They keep track of successes and failures in school programs and are inclined to move rather than help fix a school. A new generational group, called the Millennials, is just entering the teaching and parenting arenas with new values and needs. Their impact is yet to be seen.

Myth

Students do not really need to have their parents involved in order to be successful in school.

Reality

Several recent studies that have included interviews with adolescents and young adolescents have led researchers to conclude that

- Both resident and nonresident fathers who are involved with their children's schools provide significant educational advantages that are not realized when only mothers participate in school activities (Starr, 1998).

- Students are 39 percent less likely to repeat a grade and 50 percent less likely to be suspended or expelled if their nonresident fathers participate in even one in-school activity. However, nearly 70 percent of nonresident fathers and 50 percent of fathers in two-parent families are not involved in school-related activities (Starr, 1998).

- School climate has a significant impact on the degree of father involvement, particularly in Grades 6–12.

- Students in two-parent families are 43 percent more likely to get mostly A's if their fathers are highly involved in their schools (Starr, 1998).

- There is an even greater link between student achievement and parent engagement at home than there is between student achievement and parent engagement at school (Finn, 1998; Wang, Hartel, & Walberg, 1993).

- The at-home activities that appear to make the most significant difference include helping students organize their time and monitoring their use of time, helping with homework, and discussing school matters with the children (Finn, 1998).

- When parents are involved, students achieve more regardless of socioeconomic status, ethnic or racial background, or the parents' education level (National PTA, 2004).

- Student behaviors, such as alcohol use, violence, and antisocial behavior decrease as parent involvement increases.

- Both middle school and senior high school students whose parents remain involved make better transitions, maintain the quality of their work, and develop realistic plans for their future. Students whose parents are not involved, on the other hand, are more likely to drop out of school (National PTA, 2004).

Case Study #3

He is a 60-year-old grandfather who has just assumed legal guardianship of his son's four teenagers. The father of the teens has just been sentenced to life in prison for a violent crime. The teens had been left to fend for themselves under the care of their father, but the grandfather has some pretty strict rules about school and behavior.

There has been an immediate confrontation over homework, school attendance, and respect of others' property. The kids have been moved from a large city to a new school in the grandfather's small town. Two of the boys are interested in sports, but have never been eligible to play because of poor grades. The two girls would like to get involved with music, but have no idea what they can do.

Myth

Grandparents are no different than parents when it comes to school involvement.

Reality

More and more grandparents are raising children and are overwhelmed by the expectations of the school. According to data from the 2005 U.S. Census, there are more than four million children under 18 years of age being raised by a grandparent. They are often still working to support a new family structure and need additional support themselves. It may have been many years since they went to school, making them intimidated by the changes in education that have occurred. The national organization AARP has a special Web site and materials for grandparents raising grandchildren (http://www.aarp.org).

Case Study #4

They are immigrant parents who speak Spanish as their first language and limited English. They travel from Texas to Michigan to harvest crops. The children all speak English and have been successful in the schools where they have been enrolled. They attend a special summer school so that they do not get too far behind with all of their transitions. It is not unusual for them to be in three or four schools each year. The parents would love to have their children break the cycle of poverty and graduate from high school. They do not know how to converse with the school about their needs because they do not feel comfortable going to the school.

They have tried having the mother stay in one location with the kids while the father travels for work, but they found that they cannot survive on one income.

They feel overwhelmed with work, travel, and the lack of basic necessities of life.

Myth

There is no difference in race and ethnicity when it comes to parent involvement.

Reality

Parents who do not speak English are less likely than other parents to attend a general school meeting or school event, or to volunteer or serve on a committee.

Hispanic and non-Hispanic black students are less likely to have parents who attend school events or who volunteer their time compared with non-Hispanic white students (Henderson & Berla, 1994).

"Because of cultural differences, many parents are not familiar with the expectations of their children's schools and don't understand how to go about getting involved, even if they want to. Some parents lack the educational background or skills they feel they need to interact with teachers and staff. For others, their own negative experiences as students make them uncomfortable going to the school" (Aronson, 1996, p. 58). However, many schools with large numbers of non-English-speaking parents hold family literacy programs in the school, providing fathers and mothers with opportunities to increase their own language abilities while becoming familiar with the school that their child attends every day.

When parents of high school students who are low income, minority, or immigrant, attend meetings at the school that provide basic information about college entrance processes, SAT preparation, financial aid, and course placement, parents begin to imagine their adolescent as a college student, start to ask questions of the school, and build support groups with other parents. Youth whose parents get involved in this process are more apt to graduate high school and attend college (Kreider, Caspe, Kennedy, & Weiss, 2007).

When parents from diverse communities are invited to serve on formal leadership committees in the school, their children benefit. For example, higher levels of Latino parent representation on local school councils in

Chicago have been associated with a substantial increase in the number of Latino youth meeting academic standards (Marshall, 2006).

The four case studies presented in this chapter typify the parents and caregivers of today. The variable that seems to connect them all has been repeatedly researched and found to be true. Parent involvement with the school makes a significant impact on the attitude, attendance, and achievement of students (Henderson & Berla, 1994). Unfortunately, schools still struggle with parent involvement because they use traditional models of parent involvement and believe in some ancient myths. Other myths involve perceptions of roles. Who does what?

Myth

Teachers say, "Parents of today do the same things they did when I was in school."

Reality

The typical parents of today may not be able to participate in the traditional parent activities of past generations. Volunteering during the school day, attending PTO meetings, attending conferences and other school events, and having accurate information about their child may be impossible for many parents. Whereas parents 50 years ago concentrated on shaping character in their children and focused on respect, responsibility, and resourcefulness, the parents of today want those characteristics plus children with high grades, high self-esteem, and instant success.

Although they can still help monitor homework (which seems to be the variable that makes all the difference in how much homework is done), encourage their children to read, and insist on school attendance, there are often circumstances today that get in the way of these basic activities. For example, if a parent is at work while the children are doing their homework, who will monitor that process to see that it is done? As children get older, they are often left with the oldest sibling, who must feed the family and act as a surrogate parent. Their own homework is left until everyone else is cared for.

Myth

There is no correlation between teaching and parent involvement.

Reality

Teachers of students with highly involved parents tend to give greater attention to those students, and they tend to identify problems that might inhibit student learning at earlier stages (Zill & Nord, 1994). For example, many parents connect with teachers by e-mail, and schools have purchased programs that allow parents access to their child's progress on a daily basis. Parents who have Internet capabilities can immediately contact a teacher if their child is having problems. The issue is one of access and communication skills rather than availability or interest. Parents do not have to go to the school to see the teacher, but they can still get the necessary information to help their child.

More principals are e-mailing parents as well. When there is a school emergency or a last-minute meeting, principals today are apt to write rather than phone parents.

When parents ask their adolescents, "What happened in school today?" the most common response is "nothing." Shutting down the rumor mill and knowing that parents have accurate information about good and bad news is a real benefit from the use of technology.

Because student backpacks can contain months of parent notices, an e-mail from the school may ensure that parents know about meetings and class project requirements. Most schools that use e-mail to communicate with parents simply ask for addresses at the beginning of school (Delisio, 2003).

Myth

Schools do not legally have to involve parents.

Reality

The No Child Left Behind Act (2002) mandates that parents be informed of how they can become involved in school improvement efforts and provided with local report cards of schools in their district to help guide their involvement. If a school is receiving Title I funding, it is required to have written policies, annual meetings, and training on parent involvement. Schools must build and increase parent involvement programs. (see http://www.ed.gov/parents/academic/involve/nclbguide/parents guide.pdf).

Parents of children in a school that is not making adequate yearly progress must be offered options such as transfers and outside supplemental services.

Myth

Parents understand how schools work and what their rights are as parents.

Reality

"A large part of the reason why parents feel so frustrated when they encounter problems at school is because we don't know the rules of the game. We don't know what our rights are as parents, we have no inkling of what our children are entitled to as students of the school district, we have no idea what the school policies dictate, and we don't know where to find the resources that are available to us. Consequently, we are easily intimidated, misled, bewildered, and frustrated when it comes to demanding that our children be treated fairly" (Public School Parents Network, p. 1).

Case Study #5

A group of seventh-grade parents was meeting with the principal as an advisory council when one of them said, "I certainly had a great time at the parent day yesterday, but I did not get to see any of you. I guess our kids have different schedules." The other parents asked, "What parent day?" It seems that their kids had worked very hard to ensure that the notices and information did not go home. The principal realized that the process of sending notes home with students was not working and rescheduled another day so that the majority of parents could come. She also talked with students and parents to get their input into how the day might be most useful for all involved. Students were not afraid to have their parents in school—they were afraid to have their peers see their parents in school and be perceived as "immature" among their peers. It is essential that principals get student input into parent activities in the school.

Myth

Middle and high school students do not want their parents to know what is going on in school or to be involved.

Reality

There are some students who would rather not have their parents involved in school because they are participating in risky behaviors and do not want to get caught. Those who check in at their first-period class and then skip the rest of the day do not want their parents informed. Others are ambivalent, but most students want their parents to get good news from the school and to be present for events involving the student. Much depends on what the involvement will be.

Middle school students, who are going through the "my parents are so embarrassing phase" would rather not see their parents in the building and will even ask to be dropped off a block away from school in the morning. That behavior usually changes with maturity and the realization that everyone has embarrassing parents.

Myth

An open house is the best way to give today's parents necessary information at the beginning of the school year.

Reality

Many parents do not come to the open house because it is information overload.

One middle school of 600 students had a goal of 100 percent participation at its "Back to School" night held the second week of school each year. Attendance had been about 60 percent in the past and the same types of parents seemed to be missing. There were many assumptions on the part of both parents and teachers about why parents did not attend. When a teacher asked her students whether their parents were planning on attending, one student said, "No, they won't come because they don't know anyone and they don't want to sit and listen that long." When this was relayed to the principal, a committee of parents, students, and teachers was formed to organize a Back to School night with a different purpose and tone.

What transpired was later replicated in hundreds of middle schools:

- Parents were informed and invited to attend with their students. Because the invitations were handmade by the students in one of their classes, the parents read them.

- Entire families were invited, which meant that parents did not have to get babysitters.

- When the family arrived at the school, they were given three different colored cards that each had a number on it.

- The cards were coded red, yellow, and blue. There was a corresponding activity for each card. If the card had a blue 1, the family went to the blue activity, which was held in the gym. There, families participated in a few basic exercises in the new fitness program. They played two new games, and after 20 minutes, they were sent to the location of the number on their second card. If the card was red, they went to the media center, where they used markers and fabric to create a family quilt square that was later stitched into an all-school quilt. The final card was yellow; that activity was held in the cafeteria, where everyone was served ice cream and other snacks.

- ◆ Teachers and administrators were stationed in each location to meet and greet parents and families. They answered any questions that parents had but did not make formal presentations.
- ◆ As families left, they were given a reminder notice of the curriculum night that would occur in two weeks. On that night, they could walk through their child's schedule and meet the teachers. Most came back to attend curriculum night.
- ◆ The tone of the school was invitational, and word spread that Back to School night had been a fun family night out. Parents who visited the school for the first time with their student were not intimidated by the information they received, and they got a glimpse into the school environment.

There are many success stories about schools that have adjusted their traditional Back to School night to meet the needs of the parents of today.

Myth

Parents and teachers share a common language and goals in working with students.

Reality

Teachers who understand the developmental characteristics of young adolescents and high school students are able to help parents understand when behaviors are normal or abnormal.

They may spend as much or more time with the student than the parent does, and they are often the first to notice significant behavioral changes if the student is consistently in school. The behaviors that teachers see in school may or may not be visible at home. Almost every school has a typical student who does his or her homework at home under the supervision of a parent, then leaves it on the bus, loses it, or simply does not remember to hand it in. Late work lowers grades, and parents usually respond that the teacher must be thinking of another student or must have lost the work. Though this is fairly normal behavior for many students, behavioral change will come when the parents trust the teachers and work together to help the student get the work handed in.

Teachers are often the first to notice when a student has come to class having used alcohol or drugs. Parent denial is usually the first response to this situation, and the teacher must be willing to approach the situation in the context of a helping relationship rather than a disciplinary matter. Only when teachers and parents assume the role of partners can real behavior change occur in the student. Students are quite skilled at telling both parents and teachers what they want to hear. Too often, parents think that teachers do not care, and teachers think that parents are following the advice on child rearing given by President Harry Truman when he said, "The best way to give advice to your children is to find out what they want, and then advise them to do it."

In addition to informing parents of behavioral changes, teachers can help parents get involved with the curriculum by giving them previews of upcoming information and soliciting help with certain units of study. For example, one high school wanted to expand its career education program by having students shadow a person working in a particular profession. The logistics of that program were enormous, so the school asked parents to help. Hundreds of parents volunteered to be shadowed, supervise students in a multiple shadow situation, or contact people to come in as speakers if they had jobs that could not be shadowed for safety's sake.

Another school wanted to increase its offerings in the arts and music by holding a weeklong arts festival. Teachers sent home to parents a request for participation or help in finding participants. The school was overwhelmed with the response, and the students had more than 100 workshops from different artists and musicians to choose from during that week. The majority of the organizational work was done by parents.

Some parents volunteered for the entire week, while others were able to work for only an hour or two. When high school and middle school teachers tell parents exactly what kind of help they need, they will get it. Parents of students at those levels need very concrete ways of becoming involved. They also need concrete information about parenting styles, teaching methods, and school curriculum. They need to be given a working vocabulary for education. One eighth-grade student was sick with worry about the transition to high school. His parents had not completed high school but were very eager to have their son do so. When asked what he was so worried about, he said that the high school counselor had said that next year his grade-point average (GPA) would start to count. Not knowing what a GPA was, the student asked his parents, who also did not know. When the student finally asked an advisor, he and his parents were very relieved to know that a GPA was something you earned, not something you brought or bought.

Educators must identify terms that might be confusing to parents before many of these myths can be put to rest. The goal of improving achievement for all students can be met more effectively and efficiently if parents and teachers work as partners. Parents must understand the choices that their child faces and learn all of the options that are available. When students are choosing classes for high school, parents must understand the difference between required and suggested courses, between college preparatory and vocational courses, and the ramifications of each choice.

The key to finding reality in the myths of parent–school connections is communication. Students need support for their learning from the adults who are raising them and the adults who are teaching them. There is no such thing as a "typical" parent today—parents have different sets of values and needs than parents did even 20 years ago.

What students past and present need from their parents is

- Communication about themselves and the family
- Communication about expectations and beliefs
- Compassion for themselves and others
- Consideration for time, space, and ability
- Consistency in expectations
- Consistent models of positive adult behavior
- Cautions and skills for dealing with the local and faraway world
- Choices that inspire success
- Collaboration on projects for home, school, and self
- Commitment to be there when needed
- Hope for the future
- Fairness

No matter the age, race, economic status, or gender of parents today, those who send their children to school agree on what they need from the school:

- Communication about the expectations and programs of the school
- Communication about their student on a regular basis
- Compassion for their job as parents
- Consideration of their time, space, and abilities
- Consistency in expectations
- Fairness
- Choices that inspire success as parents
- A common vocabulary about schooling that they can understand
- Collaboration on goals and projects that improve schools
- A curriculum that is age appropriate, challenging, and connected to the real world
- Consistent models of positive adult behavior from teachers and administrators

Schools that recognize the needs of both students and their parents have significantly improved parent participation in the school and the learning of their students.

Taking the Dare:
About that Parent Who Dared Us to Teach His Kid.

On the first page of the chapter you were introduced to a challenging parent and his son. That student who had not been to school for eight years and his father became the special challenge of the school staff and principal that year. The shop teacher discovered that the young man had a tremendous talent for woodworking and could do math related to measurement. The English teacher found woodworking manuals that the boy could learn to read. Because he had been driving without a license, he also eagerly perused the driver's education training manual. Other teachers worked with him after school to help him catch up in social studies and science. When it looked like he might have a chance to win the regional competition in woodworking, the principal got the student's father involved in the process. Because the father was familiar with the boy's talent in woodworking, he was comfortable coming to the school for those events. It took the father three years to realize that his son could learn, but eventually he came to respect his son as a person. The boy won the state competition in woodworking and graduated in three years. This school staff took the dare that is offered so often today.

2

The Roles of Parents, Educators, and Students

There was a scheduled faculty meeting after school following Back to School night the previous evening. The teachers were buzzing about the lack of parent turnout. The principal calculated that less than half of the students had someone represent them at the event. Teachers grumbled that the parents who showed up really didn't need to—it was the parents who didn't show who should have been there. The faculty intimated that it really hadn't been worth their extra time at school away from their own families. Some even threatened to "be sick" for the next parent event. The principal listened to the grousing and knew that she should try to rein in the teachers' negative views of parent involvement—or rather, noninvolvement—in their school.

So, what to do? Actually, the problem now sits squarely in the laps of the educational staff. The administrators and teachers must find out why parents neglected to come; get ideas from parents, teachers, and students; and set up a plan with lots of ideas, options, and enthusiasm.

What follows in this chapter are descriptions of roles that administrators, teachers, parents, and students can assume in successful home–school collaborations.

The Roles of Administrators

The following is a list of tasks that an administrator can undertake to foster effective parent involvement practices:

- Establish a climate of collaboration and model excitement for home–school relationships
- Set up a task force on parent involvement
- Oversee a written policy for parent involvement
- Devise an effective routine for ongoing communication between home and school
- Provide training for teachers and parents—all must realize the importance of parent involvement
- Provide research and strategies to teachers
- Hire teachers who want to work with parents
- Involve parents and teachers in designing the initiatives
- Evaluate the policy and practices, including the teachers' active involvement and reasons for parent involvement or noninvolvement
- Establish a parent resource center

A Climate of Collaboration

First and foremost, school administrators are responsible for establishing a climate in which parent involvement is valued. Parent involvement is not a program that is just nice to support; it is now a requirement mandated by the No Child Left Behind Act. However, it shouldn't be viewed as just a political ploy to be disdained and reluctantly implemented. Successful parent involvement programs can have important benefits for student learning, thus making teachers' jobs easier! Administrators must ensure that faculty, staff, parents, and students understand the importance and priority of parent involvement practices and establish an environment that supports them.

The tone set by the entrance to the school and the main office staff is critical. The authors have witnessed—and experienced!—occasions when parents were treated as annoyances. Such an initial impression drives parents away, or worse, turns them into adversaries. Look at the signs that welcome visitors to the school. Are they, in fact, welcoming? Sure, because of safety standards, visitors need to be directed to the main office, but in what way? Here are some examples. See for yourself the tone they set:

- All visitors must report to the main office.
- Ring the bell and wait for admittance.

- ◆ Welcome to our school. We value our educational community and our students' safety. Please visit our main office so that we may assist you.

Next, critique how visitors are actually treated upon arrival at the office. How long must they wait for assistance? Who greets them, and what is said? Administrators are responsible for ensuring that parents feel valued as they interact with school personnel. Consider how reluctant a parent would be to join a parent conference if he or she felt uncomfortable merely bringing in forgotten lunch money!

Administrators can begin by providing pertinent and practical research to parents and teachers. Perhaps all teachers could read the same information, then discuss it in team or faculty meetings. The principal should also establish a resource room for parent involvement (perhaps a lending library that includes videos on parenting skills, available in the languages used by families of the school's students) where teachers and parents can get ideas. The principal should also build a parent advocacy group with family, educator, and community representation. The first task of this group would be to carry out a needs assessment to discover what and how parent involvement can be established or improved in the local area.

A Written Policy

Why written? So that it's not an option and so that there is no ambiguity about what is expected. Administrators should assemble a group of teachers, students (if age-level appropriate), and parents to write a succinct policy regarding school–family–community collaboration. This policy should be specific enough that teachers know exactly what is expected of them and can be evaluated on their efforts. When writing the policy, consider the mandates of the No Child Left Behind Act.

Communication Routines

Often, trouble is stirred up because of miscommunication. Who sends home what? When? How many different communications are going home at different intervals in the week and school year? Many students spend different days of the week with alternating parent custodians. If communications go out randomly, it is too easy for the information to get lost. Parents should know when to expect school communications and know whom to call if they have questions or concerns. Again, administrators need to design procedures in cooperation with the educational staff. For example, many schools now are sending a communications packet home with each student every Wednesday. Parents know to expect it. All information that needs to be signed, acknowledged, or shared goes in that packet.

Administrators also can make sure that use of the school's Web site is effective. Does the Web site foster communication or make it difficult? The authors have been amazed at the number of schools that do not list pertinent e-mail addresses for parents to use. What is the point of having a Web site if parents are not given specific details of how to communicate with the appropriate school personnel?

Training

This role is a big deal, and it is often neglected. We may expect teachers and caregivers to interact, but we rarely teach them how. Many of the parents who "need" to interact with school personnel do not do so because they don't know what good it will do or why it is important; they have communications problems; they have cultural, schedule-related, or health issues or other life circumstances that preclude their involvement; or they have trust issues. Educators need to learn what parents' issues are and devise ways of fostering parent and teacher learning about those issues. This role necessitates that administrators know what concerns impede home–school collaboration and design sessions to improve it. For example, one middle school principal did some demographic research and determined that many of the parents of his students were quite young. He then designed a "Masters in Parenting" series of workshops (which were videotaped and put in the lending library) to help parents understand the developmental needs of their children. Babysitting was available for younger children, and students from the school were integrally involved in activities provided on the days and evenings that the sessions were held.

Similarly, administrators must not assume that teachers know how or why it is important to build strong home–school relationships. Teachers may also need instruction on language or cultural idiosyncrasies that may be affecting collaborative efforts. Administrators must determine local needs, design the structure, and attend the sessions in order to model the importance of the workshop content! Designing, facilitating, and "selling" professional development sessions to the professional staff are important tasks of school administrators.

Hiring

This role is simple. Principals need to add questions to the interviewing process to determine whether a potential candidate for a teaching position would support or, optimally, encourage home–school collaboration. Which candidates know how to do it? If principals start asking such questions in interviews, surely teacher preparation programs will provide increasingly meaningful instruction on the topic.

Collaborative Program Design

Needless to say, collaborative programs must be collaboratively designed and carried out! Administrators are responsible for recruiting and facilitating participants in the needs assessment, design, implementation, and evaluation of any collaborative endeavor. Parents and caregivers must be surveyed in order to determine their needs, desires, and concerns. Too often, programs are designed without family or student input. Any successful endeavor recognizes that all constituents must be represented in the needs assessment and design of the collaborative effort.

Evaluation

This is the most frequently neglected part of the effort. How do we know whether the plan and strategies are effective and whether integral participants are doing what is expected of them? Perhaps administrators could collaborate with local universities to design an evaluative component of the home–school collaboration project. Regardless of sophistication, the administrator of the program must know whether it is working, why it is or is not working, and who is helping or hindering the process. In the authors' opinion, part of a teacher's annual evaluation ought to refer to efforts to enhance home–school collaboration.

Parent Resource Center

Many parents don't know how to support the academic environment. They don't know how or what to communicate or what to do. They are confused by the increasingly complex curricular demands. Many were not provided with strong parental models themselves. Where do they go for help and information in a comfortable nonjudgmental setting? The answer is a parent resource center—which may be housed at the school, at the local library, in a local community center, in a place of worship, or in all of these places and more. The point is that school administrators cannot afford the luxury (or delusion) that it is someone else's responsibility to educate families about the importance, roles, and responsibilities that are necessary.

The Roles of Teachers

Teachers are at the heart of successful parent involvement programs. They have the most interaction with students and their families, and they know what resources are necessary to support parent–school interactions. Teachers must buy in to comprehensive parent involvement programs and be willing to spend the time and effort necessary to establish, evaluate, and then maintain effective strategies. It is important that teachers not only are enthusiastic about establishing and maintaining effective parent involvement programs but also have the knowledge and skills to help them succeed. The roles of teachers include the following:

- Communicating with parents and caregivers about the academic, social, and behavioral needs and progress of students.

- Attending (enthusiastically!) professional development experiences that help them learn about and respond to the special needs of students, including language difficulties; familial, cultural, or demographic idiosyncrasies of local families; and learning disabilities and behavioral disorders.

- Helping families work with academic and behavioral goals at home to support school success.

- Collaborating with administrators, parents, students (if age appropriate), and colleagues regarding written policies, expectations, and evaluation of collaborative efforts.

Communicating

The communication goals of teachers should go far beyond merely reporting a grade or a student's lack of progress. Educators need to think first of preventive communication—that is, what kinds of communications between home and school may prevent academic or behavioral problems in school? The National PTA (1998) terms such communications "partnering," a sharing of information between educators and parents. Early communications are necessary to set a positive and collaborative atmosphere between home and school. Teachers need to let parents know that it is in their child's best interest that home and school work together. These first communications also provide parents with means of contact, ways of supporting the academic program in the home, and information regarding the year's academic goals. Parents (and students) should be familiar with what the academic goals are and what success entails.

Communications with the home should be welcoming and respectful. The creation of a culture of effective collaboration lies in the ability of teachers to encourage parents to want to be involved. Obviously, this recommendation implies that teachers communicate with the home beyond criticizing a student's work or behavior.

To that end, teachers must organize a structure to keep examples of students' work that show their progress toward stated objectives or standards. This work is used to show concretely the academic areas of strength and those in need of further attention. Parents then know specifically what their child must do to improve. Too often, educators tend to show the results of test scores—a performance that is over and done with. Once a student fails a test, what are parents to do? Conferences and communications held earlier in a semester can be much more valuable than those held at report card time. (See the student-led conference section under Students' Roles).

Attending

Once teachers understand and embrace home–school collaboration, they should seek out professional development opportunities that will help them reach out to families of diverse backgrounds and means. More and more professional literature and professional conference presentations are addressing this area of schooling, and teachers need to avail themselves of the new research and ideas. Some planning, team meeting, and faculty meeting times should be used to discuss the literature and the benefits of suggested policies and programs.

Times have changed! American classrooms are more diverse than ever before. We can no longer accept the luxury of thinking that our students come from similar backgrounds, cultures, and values. Something as small as a misunderstanding over eye contact can taint a relationship between school and home. Some cultures view eye contact as a threat or as a sign of disrespect, so telling a student to "look at me when I'm talking to you" can garner unwanted consequences. Teachers, then, are encouraged to research the cultures that are represented in their classrooms and to ask students and families how they are most comfortable communicating.

Educators need to be able to converse knowledgeably with parents about a variety of difficulties that youngsters bring to school, and they must learn ways of dealing effectively with a myriad of learning challenges. For example, teachers must now know how to approach children and families who are coping with the symptoms of the autism spectrum, including Asperger's syndrome. Therefore, teachers need to understand federal and state laws regarding learning difficulties and be comfortable helping to design and carry out learning accommodations. Obviously, because parents are an integral part of this process, teachers need to know how to work with parents to reach mutually agreeable terms.

Professional development workshops on conferencing techniques, including how to organize an effective program of student-led conferences, are imperative. Teachers need to understand how something as simple as the seating arrangement at a conference can affect the tone and effectiveness of the meeting. Setting up seats so that parents and teachers are on two opposing sides is not a great idea. Circles give the impression that "we're all in this together" and are not as intimidating as square tables. Teachers should sit with the parents, not at their desk or lab table.

Helping

During the course of the school year, teachers can also provide families with specific means of supporting the academic program. Often parents want to help, but they don't know how. Teachers need to provide such information. Web sites, homework hotlines, sharing of curriculum goals, video series, and workshops can all help. Epstein and Herrick (1991) found that sending learning packets home over the summer helped with students' academic achievement during the following school year. Especially as children move from elementary to middle school, parents need more information regarding the content of the curriculum. We know that parents often feel intimidated by some of the academic requirements starting in middle school.

Many parents could also benefit from behavioral and management advice from educators. And teachers could benefit from parents' experiences in dealing with their child's difficulties. Parents who had poor adult role models themselves may not know how to deal with aggressive youngsters or teenagers who are asserting their independence. Helping to establish limits in the home that complement those in school will create more consistency for the students who need it most.

Too often, parent communications are viewed as the negative consequences of poor student behavior or performance. It is incumbent on educators to change that perspective!

Collaborating

It is an integral part of a teacher's role to help write and evaluate policies for and expectations of home–school partnerships. Many schools are including such participation in teachers' annual performance ratings. In one school, the teachers decided to open the school library on certain evenings and provide a "teacher on call" to help with homework or other academic needs. Because the idea originated from the teachers and they understood the value of such time spent, most teachers agreed. They set up a schedule so that each teacher had to volunteer only about an hour a month. It reaped great rewards, however, as increasing numbers of families and students took advantage of the time in the library. Younger children in the family were also introduced to the library and the world of reading at an earlier age than might otherwise have happened.

Teachers need to study the roles of parents and design ways of including parents at each level. Some parents want to help in the classroom but don't necessarily know what they can do. Working parents may want to be involved but can't come to school during the day. Teachers need to help parents understand what they can do to support the school despite economic, social, and cultural limitations. One of the reasons that elementary schools enjoy more parent involvement is that parents better understand their role at that level. Once youngsters enter middle school, parents lose confidence in the roles they can play. Teachers need to help.

Just as teachers are expected to help design policies and programs for home–school partnerships, so, too, must they be included in the evaluation and readjustment of the initiatives. Teachers are where the rubber meets the road, so they must be involved in maintaining a high level of success for family involvement practices.

The Roles of Parents

Not all parents have the same interests or skills to participate fully in school programs. Most researchers (see e.g., Epstein, 1991; Chrispeels, 1996; National PTA, 1998, 2004) divide the roles of parents into five or six categories:

- ◆ **Parenting:** Parents are supported in their understanding of their child's developmental and academic characteristics and needs.
- ◆ **Communicating:** Caregivers and school professional staff communicate about school programs and student progress.
- ◆ **Volunteering:** Caregivers serve as helpers and audience members.
- ◆ **Learning at home:** Parents know what to do to help with homework and academic goal setting; parents and kids talk about curriculum content
- ◆ **Decision making:** Parents participate in school governance and advocacy
- ◆ **Collaborating with the community:** Community, schools, and families work together to provide resources to support kids, families, and schools

Note that the hierarchy of involvement does not commit a parent to a high level of interaction within the school. Our goal should be to involve caregivers at levels that are possible and reasonable given the home circumstances. For example, language barriers may preclude sophisticated levels of interaction but may be quite possible for less complex tasks.

Many other examples of involvement exist, but as Brough has pointed out, "Factors consistent among the models are that schools assess the effectiveness of their own efforts at developing home-school partnerships, determine why uninvolved parents are not assuming a role in school activities, build a rationale and commitment for getting the parents and families involved, and make a concerted effort to reach all families" (1997, p. 269). Providing a variety of ways for parents and caregivers to support student learning is key to successful programs.

Parenting

Educators have the benefit of college classes and professional workshops regarding the developmental needs and characteristics of the students they are teaching. Therefore, they often can better respond to a child's needs. Most parents do not have the benefit of such instruction, and many lack a proper parental role model themselves. We cannot assume that parents know the developmental stages of their youngsters or understand how to respond to increasing demands for independence. Therefore, it is important for school personnel to provide such information to parents in their local community. Some schools hire speakers, videotape them, and send the tapes to interested parents. Certainly, a library of child development literature is necessary, but not all parents can or will come to the school to access the information. Therefore, schools need to find means of providing this valuable information to adults in the community, including those who speak languages other than English.

Communicating

Parents partner with educators to focus on the progress and needs of their children. Parents need to know whom and how to contact school liaisons. At a minimum, parents and teachers share information regarding the welfare of the students. Face-to-face meetings seem to be more effective than notes and e-mails, but certainly the latter are more convenient.

One of the most important roles for parents is attendance at parent–teacher conferences. Parents should know how to prepare for the conferences and what to expect. Teachers should be open to listening to parents rather than just talking at them, and parents should be open to sharing information and considering suggestions made by the teacher. The "we" dialogue used in effective conferences shows all parties that they are part of a team working for the success of the child. If the school is too intimidating for some parents, consider holding the conferences at a community venue.

Volunteering

Volunteering can mean more to parents than being band boosters, fund-raisers, and homeroom mothers. Parents can offer a variety of skills and interests that can benefit the academic program. Not only can parents come to the school to give a presentation, read to the students, monitor small group work, or help with clerical duties, they can help at home as well. Parents can help with word processing, organize files, network with other parents to get them involved, or host a small neighborhood event centered around school. Many parents want to help the school but don't know how. If parents receive a list of tasks that can be done in different amounts of time and during different times of the day, more parents are likely to volunteer. The point to remember is that it's not the type of volunteering that is important. Kids just need to see concretely that their parents consider school important enough to spend time volunteering.

Learning at Home

Parents can be given suggestions for how to reinforce the academic program in the home. Some schools actually provide Web sites and tutoring sessions for parents as well as students. This seems to be especially important over the summer months, to prevent some of the academic decline that so often accompanies the long vacation from school (Epstein & Herrick, 1991).

Burkhardt (2004) suggests a "parent writing conference." This interaction involves the student selecting pieces of his or her own writing and placing them in a folder. The student then writes a few questions, comments, or observations about the writing before meeting with his or her parents. After a discussion of the writing, the student makes reflections in a writing journal, and parents may add their own comments. This is a wonderful, nonthreatening task for parents and students to do together. A side benefit is that it sometimes prompts the television or video games to be turned off.

Decision Making

Some parents want a voice in the governance and structure of the schools' programs. Typically, parents are interested in programs for the gifted, as well as sports, music, and other organizations. Usually these are parents who understand the system and want to advocate for programs that are of interest to their kids. But now, with many schools reviewing grade organization and evaluation practices, it may be time to get parent input in other parts of the school environment as well. Again, some parents may not know what opportunities exist for their input, so administrators need to get the word out. The more parents understand the daily complexities of the school, the more likely they are to support it. If parents want to spend an abundance of time on school issues, they should be encouraged to run for a seat on the school board.

Working with the Community

Let's face it—media reports about education are less than glowing these days. Parents can help to provide a more positive picture by getting out in the community to share their optimism. One middle school worked with parents on the design of a new middle school program. Parents who were involved in the design were given buttons that said, "Ask me about our middle school," and they wore the buttons around town. These parents were stopped in the mall and the grocery store and asked about current rumors and concerns. The participating parents were able to tell the "real story," and they were able to talk with the media about the terrific experiences that were being planned for the community's young adolescents.

Another school solicited area businesses and was able to get small grants to help support special school programs. One local insurance company even provided airfare for several teachers to attend a national conference to learn more about educating at-risk students.

We have a variety of talents and resources in the community that parents can help us tap into.

The Roles of Students

Students, too, should be aware that they have a role in fostering effective collaboration between home and school. Too often, we tend to make students carriers of information rather than designing and describing important roles with them. Wise teachers enlist the help of their students in establishing means of getting their parents involved. Some students, especially in the middle grades, may act as if they don't want their parents to interact with their teachers, but, in fact, they do—they just may not admit it in front of their peers.

There's an old joke that recounts a conversation between a mom and her son. She asks, "What did you learn in school today?" He replies, "I don't know; the teacher forgot to tell us." These words hold some truth. Sometimes kids need a summary of school events or a reflective journal to take home. Teachers could help the kids with conversation starters to initiate a family discussion about their school experience. The use of agenda books has certainly increased in elementary and middle schools, and this gives parents a concrete source to review school happenings. High schoolers in many communities are now being asked to keep a reflective journal that goes home every day. Adolescents can be encouraged to share their thoughts at home, which may foster important dialogue.

One of the main tasks of students in home–school partnerships is to lead a conference about their academic progress and their demeanor in school. Students should be encouraged to keep a portfolio of their work in each subject, reflect on each piece, and determine further goals for themselves to share with their teachers and caregivers.

Here are some suggestions for the student-led conference:

- The teacher and students decide which standards and objectives need to be shared with parents.

- Students select representative pieces of work that demonstrate their progress toward the objectives. They reflect on each piece by evaluating their strengths and areas that need improvement.

- After reviewing their portfolios and reflections of their work, students design goals for themselves.

- Students also think about what information their parents would like to know.

- Students script the conference in the sequence they will discuss the contents of the portfolio. Some teachers even allow time for rehearsals.

- Students present their findings, reflections, and goals to their parents at the conference.

- A contract is formed—what the student will do, what the parents will do, and what the teacher will do to ensure mastery of the goals. This is established after a healthy discussion of the students' identified goals.

- About a month after the conference, students write and send home a letter about their progress, reminding parents of the contract.

- Students and parents evaluate the success of the conference and share this information with the teacher.

Many parents will attend school functions that spotlight their own children. Having student work displayed, student recitations given, or other means of enticing parents to the school to see their children in action are successful ways of bringing in parents.

Conclusion

Teaching and learning is more difficult than it ever has been. In this age of high-stakes testing and accountability, parents and teachers must realize that the best way to nurture academic success is to work together. Call it a "collaboration of caring," if you will. Students need to understand that parents and teachers are on the same team and on their side. Too often, parent involvement programs are an afterthought. Relationships are too complex to leave them to chance. Everyone must be confident of his or her role; everyone must participate; and schools must assume the responsibility of concretely showing parents that their participation matters.

3

Developing a Culture of Participation: Strategies for Involving All Parents

Chapter 1 presented evidence from the research regarding the need for parent involvement and the rationale behind its importance. At this point, there is no need to further examine why the involvement of parents is so vitally important for all schools. This chapter will begin the process of sharing ideas that have proven their merit over time in schools across the country. This chapter will deal with all parents as a generic group. Chapters 4, 5, and 6 will deal with subsets of this group. The strategies and ideas shared in this chapter apply to all parents. All of the suggestions have worked somewhere in some school and could work in any building if given the appropriate attention. All schools need the support of the home in order to meet the growing needs of students. A fundamental premise that educators need to realize is that we hope we can enlist the support of parents, but we really shouldn't care one way or another about whom we recruit. The labels "parent," "step-parent," "guardian," "foster parent," "legal custodian," "coach," or "grandparent" should not matter whatsoever. The ultimate goal is to find an adult who is responsible, who knows the student, and who is willing to help the school care for the student. If the school is able to connect with somebody on the student's behalf, the chances of that student's success increase.

Parent involvement is a part of a school's total culture, and as such, it is not established over night. By the same token, this part of the culture cannot be corrected overnight either. Schools that are serious about improving parent involvement must make positive changes to their existing conditions over an extended period of time. We know that the actions, perceptions, beliefs, and attitudes of a school blend together to establish its culture, but there is more. At a recent workshop with a group of teachers, the question "What is culture?" was asked. After much discussion and brainstorming, a teacher said, "Culture is everything we say and everything we do on a daily basis to help children." After a period of silence, a second teacher added, "It is also everything we don't do and don't say that we probably should." This inclusion of all areas of the school environment caused a collective flashbulb to go off simultaneously in every head in the room. This group had established a common mind-set about school culture, and for the remainder of the workshop everything they learned and every activity they participated in reflected this new focus. As you review the suggestions and ideas in this chapter, we hope that you will do so with this type of mind-set—change your "parent culture," and you will reach more parents.

Throughout their works on invitational education, Purkey and Novak (1996) talk at length about "inviting" and "welcoming" schools. They point out that schools must be places where teachers, students, and parents want to come, and schools must be places where all groups experience success. They state, "Education is fundamentally an act of hope. This hope generates an educational vision and suggests creative means of attainment...everything in schools should invite the realizing of educational goals...this involves the people...the places...the policies...the programs...and the processes" (p.1). The authors are referring to every aspect of a school's culture. Parents are a significant part of this culture. With this idea as the foundation for our "cultural revolution" in parent involvement, the remainder of this chapter will be devoted to activities that can jump-start your change process.

The chapter is organized into five sections:

1. **Repetition:** The knowledge and ideas you may already know and need to continue using

2. **Communication:** Activities designed to connect with all parents

3. **Information:** Strategies for making sure parents are informed

4. **Education:** Opportunities for parents to learn more about the school, its programs, and their child's involvement

5. **Invitation:** Suggestions to improve the school's "welcoming quotient."

Repetition

There are dozens of organizations that have information regarding parent involvement, including the Association for Supervision and Curriculum Development, National Middle School Association, National PTA, National Association of Secondary School Principals, National Association of Elementary School Principals, Parent Institute, National School Safety Center, and the Johns Hopkins University Center on Families (see the Resources section at the back of this book for more information). Almost all of these agencies have research on why parent involvement is important and offer ways to improve your school's parent participation. This section includes some ideas from these sources and other general ideas that have been the standard at many schools for years. All of these suggestions have stood the test of time and can help create a more welcoming culture within your school.

- ◆ Always remember that the best results are achieved when interacting with parents face to face. Personal interaction is much better than telephone contacts, and it is far superior to both letters and e-mail messages. Increase the opportunities for face-to-face interactions.

- ◆ Always collect and keep data on parent involvement. Keep track of how many parents come to school, the number of parent conferences, parents' reasons for coming, and who they are. Use the numbers to compare programs, months, and parent interests and to plan your school programs accordingly.

- ◆ When parents make a special effort to attend a function or to volunteer, make sure you thank them individually, if possible, or collectively if the attendance is too large. A thank you note from a staff member reinforces the positive nature of the interaction and your commitment to parent involvement.

- ◆ Work hard to eliminate all barriers to involvement (see Chapter 4).

- ◆ Make sure the welcome signs in your hallways reflect the cultural makeup of your student body. Display signs that are written in the native languages represented by your population.

Remember and emphasize the three Fs: fun, families, and food.

- ◆ Invite parents to cosponsor clubs and organizations with teachers.

- ◆ Urge the district to implement policies that require schools to seek parent involvement. If your school leads this initiative, the school will send a message to the entire school community that it is serious about parent involvement.

- Make sure every committee within the building includes parent representation.

- Provide a parent handbook describing expectations, routines, policies, contact information, graduation requirements, and so on, to all parents. For entry grades and transition stages, educate parents about what to expect for the next few years while their student attends your school.

- Provide information that outlines your school beliefs regarding the importance of parents. Publish and distribute an "opportunities for participation" letter that ensures the school will do its part to include parents (see Appendix A).

- Supply all visitors with a courtesy comment card whenever they come to school, as many hotels and restaurants do. Use a stamped postcard with the school address preprinted on the front. Ask visitors whether they were greeted warmly, received an answer to their question, thought the school looked clean, and so on. A space for comments is very helpful. Appoint a staff person to read and respond to every card that is received. Use the cards to compile data for future decision making.

- Create parent focus groups based on parents' needs. Topics such as single parenting, raising a teenager, obesity, divorce, sexually active children, and anger management are on the minds of all parents.

- Make sure that an administrator or guidance counselor attends every parent organization meeting, whether it is a regular or a board meeting. Your attendance clearly states that the activity is a priority to the school.

- Provide multiple opportunities to chaperone school events. Always invite parents to go with their children whenever they leave school. High school students think this is unnecessary, but parents appreciate being asked anyway.

- Publish school newsletters on a regular basis (four times a year is a bare minimum). Thank parents, recognize students, publish a "What Is Right" this year column, and advertise upcoming events. If the school is organized by grade levels, departments, or teams, have each group contribute a column to the newsletter.

- Investigate and then implement the use of student-led conferences. When students do the talking, parent involvement skyrockets. This is especially effective in upper primary, middle, and high schools (see Chapter 2).

♦ Host a school health fair for all school stakeholders. Invite hospitals, doctors, health care agencies, and mental health professionals to participate or present. The exposure for the exhibitors and the service provided to parents makes this a win–win situation.

♦ At all school events, see that administrators and school leaders work the crowd. Saying hello and then standing by the door or the gate is not the same as shaking hands and asking questions about how the school year is going for parents. Use the opportunity to invite parents to participate in an upcoming activity.

♦ Sponsor game nights, open gym nights, scary movie nights, or family lock-in nights as often as possible. These informal gatherings provide ample opportunities to build relationships.

♦ A school open house held at the beginning of the year is an almost universal activity. The next time your school is planning one, try these ideas:

  • Break the activities into several smaller events by having teams, academies, or small learning communities host their own events.

  • Spread the open house over several evenings if your school is extremely large. Parents will appreciate the personalization of a smaller group.

  • Ask all neighborhood churches, synagogues, mosques, and temples to advertise the open house. They can also encourage parents to attend.

  • Give away as many door prizes as you can get donated by community businesses to parents who attend the open house.

  • Have the students handwrite a letter to their parents inviting them to attend. Young students can copy the text from a template and then personalize it with their parents' names.

♦ Search the newspaper for any mention of a student's name or any pictures (sports, girl or boy scouts, community service, churches, births of siblings) and cut out the article. Send the cutout with an short note to the parents from the school. Something like, "We saw this article about _____ and thought you may like another copy. We know you are as proud of _____ as we are."

♦ Allocate a part of the school budget as a line item for parent mailings. The delivery of report cards and progress reports by the U.S. Postal Service is a better bet than putting them in the book bag of any student.

♦ Offer summer tours, orientation meetings and summer hours so that parents who have students entering your school in the fall can familiarize themselves with room placements, hallways that may all look the same, and parking and traffic patterns.

This list is a great place to start if you intend to get serious about your "cultural revolution." The ideas and thoughts come from hundreds of schools across the country. Some of them are just meant for your school.

Communication

This section will deal with home–school communications and make suggestions on improving this aspect of your parent culture. Highly successful schools are built on honest, open, and trustworthy lines of communication. These lines run from school to home and from home to school. They allow for information to flow both ways and for parent involvement to improve. Communications should start early and occur often.

♦ Send out summer letters that are personalized by the teacher, grade level, or academy that the student will be a part of in the fall. The stale, worn-out form letter that states only what room and teacher to report to does not generate much excitement in most homes.

♦ Obtain a list of students' summer addresses and communicate with them before school begins. Teachers can inquire about summer activities and encourage their future students to read certain books or review certain concepts. The students begin to develop a relationship with the teacher before school begins.

♦ Make the school completely accessible online with e-mail addresses for all staff and individual Web pages for grades, teams, departments, and academies. Post course outlines, grading policies, project due dates, reminders, and activities on a regular basis. Have a staff member review all Web sites regularly to make sure they are updated monthly.

♦ Have departments, teams, and academies develop and distribute brochures that outline their programs and highlight the accomplishments of that group.

♦ Eliminate education jargon and abbreviations from all communications that are sent home. If parents cannot understand us, we cannot establish communications. Try to eliminate such language when talking to parents by telephone and in person as well.

- Encourage the assignment of homework that requires the student to talk to an adult and ask questions on a regular basis (weekly). Involving parents in this manner helps not only the students but the family as well.

- Develop a Listserv to manage e-mail addresses that you obtain from caretakers (home, work, friend) and send out daily announcements, activities schedules, upcoming field trips, and lunch menus electronically.

- Have a parent bulletin board placed near the main entrance of the building. Alert the parents to its existence and fill it with information and school news. This is a good place to post minutes from all committee meetings.

- Consider doing away with telephone answering machines during school hours. It may save time, but very few people enjoy listening to "Dial 1 if you want _____, dial 2 if you want _____." Adults generally want to talk to another adult. The machine eliminates the human interactions that enhance communication.

- For elementary and middle schools, establish one day of the week on which important papers are sent home for reading. Having a routine signature day encourages parents to pay particular attention on that evening. Some schools have successfully set up "Take Home Thursdays" and "Bring Back Fridays" as their standard with great success.

- Develop a relationship with somebody at the local newspaper and ask him or her to help your school distribute information. A regular, "What's Happening at _____ School" column can be effective. Send information of all types to the newspaper so it can generate articles from your ideas.

- Do the same thing with any local radio or television station in your community.

- Use parent information sheets to your advantage (see Chapter 4).

- Translate all signs, maps, and directional arrows in your building into the first languages that are spoken within your school community.

- Update your "Who Haven't We Contacted" list on a regular basis (see Chapter 4).

- Establish a resource file of parents who are willing to serve the school as volunteers. Coordinate their efforts through a staff person. The easiest way to gather this information is through the use of a parent participation form (see Appendix B).

- Develop a primary contact program (see Chapter 4).
- Call or send postcards to parents with good news about their child. Develop a simple postcard that teachers can check off and address. For example, "Dear Parents, (child's name) had a great day at school today because of (reason). We wanted to let you know. Sincerely, (Teacher's name)."
- Train and encourage all staff to use the "feel, felt, found" method when communicating with unhappy parents. The method is very simple and effective when addressing parents' concerns. After the parent has finished describing his or her displeasure, state the following:
  - "I understand how you feel. You are upset, angry, confused, sad" (whatever adjectives fit).
  - "I felt the same way when _____ happened to me." Relate a story from your life when things didn't go quite right and you had similar feelings. This statement sends the message that you understand and that you are also human.
  - Finally, say, "I had these feelings, but after I looked into things I found out that _____. Relate how a resolution was reached, how more information allowed you to see the whole picture, and encourage them to do the same.
- "Saturdays at the Store" works very well in some areas of the country and is a favorite in many rural districts. On Saturdays, many people shop at the biggest store in the county. Whether it is Wal-Mart, Big K, Big Lots, or a grocery chain, the parents show up. Encourage school staff to do likewise, and people will literally bump into one another. The Saturdays can be scheduled and parents can be notified that math teachers will be there on the first Saturday, sixth grade teachers on the second Saturday, elective teachers on the third Saturday, and so on. All the teachers need to do is go shopping and wear a button that reads, "Ask me what is great about _____ School." Parents will initiate informal discussions. This cannot be mandatory in most districts, but it works just as well with staff members who volunteer.

The suggestions in this section target the area of building parent communication opportunities. Strengthening this aspect of your parent culture will ultimately strengthen all other areas as well.

Information

It is important to ensure that when information is given by schools, it is clear, useful, and benefits both parents and students. The following ideas are suggested as ways to distribute information more efficiently.

- Create and distribute refrigerator magnets that have information such as school contact phone numbers, the school calendar, school Web site address, grading period information, and e-mail addresses. The magnet can have any or of all this information. When placed in the kitchen, it is a powerful reminder to students that school is just a phone call away.

- Place a school marquee or message board on the front lawn and change it daily. Any parent dropping off students or driving by will develop a habit of reading what is posted. Announce meetings, field trips, upcoming events, or related events, and parents will respond. Make the daily update the responsibility of one individual or class.

- Place a single copy of all currently used text books in the reference section of the public library nearest your school. Inform all parents that the books are there for use by their children. Encourage parents not to accept "I left my book at school" as an excuse for not doing homework. Just get in the car and go to the library.

- Some middle schools and high schools produce radio and television spots to promote school activities. Explore this possibility through a speech or communications class. In many communities with cable television service, the school system has its own channel for programming. If there are many schools in the district that share the available air time, personally invite the reporters and cameras to come to your school for all events so that they will have current footage when your programs are scheduled.

- Provide accurate building maps to all visitors as part of your initial greeting.

- Post directional signs in hallways that detail how to get from one point to another quickly.

Distribute free copies of the *H.E.L.P.* and *More H.E.L.P.* booklets to all middle school parents. These short pamphlets written by Judith Baenen and distributed by the National Middle School Association are an inexpensive way to inform parents of what to expect in Grades 5–8. (H.E.L.P. stands for "how to enjoy living with a preadolescent.")

- Establish a homework hotline that parents can call 24 hours a day. Have each teacher, team, or academy list the homework that was given today and will be due tomorrow. The service needs to be updated daily. Parents can then call and make sure their child really doesn't have any homework or get assignments for a student who was absent.

- Establish a homework helpline or homework huddle that students and parents can call to receive help with a homework assignment that is troubling. A teacher who can assist the caller should answer this phone number. Usually operated from 3:30 p.m. to 6:00 p.m. and staffed by a teacher who is paid a supplement, this service encourages positive communication. Parents who cannot help their children with their homework will be most thankful.

- Make sure that every parent receives a course outline, syllabus, and grade-level expectations for every class at the beginning of the year. This is extremely important at all levels of schooling, as parents cannot become partners in the educational process unless they know what we are teaching and what their students should be learning. Parents, students, and educators should be able to describe what it means to be "on grade level."

- Establish a shelf or an area in the public library, community center, or school library where parent resource materials are kept. Place books, tapes, DVDs, newsletters, committee minutes, and pamphlets regarding the school in particular and parenting in general in this collection. Inform parents of its existence and purpose and encourage its use. Allow parents to check out materials when appropriate.

- Distribute student agenda books free to all students. Include information for parents at the front and encourage parents to check the books periodically for homework assignments. If funds for the project are limited, solicit sponsors from the community or sell advertising space.

- Sponsor school days to encourage parent participation. Grandparents' Day, Cultural Awareness Day, Career Day, Mom's Day, Dad's Day, Genealogy Day, and so on are all events that can have both a learning focus and a parent involvement focus.

- Many communities have a welcome wagon organization that goes to the homes of new residents with a basket of gifts and community information. The personal touch of a face-to-face welcome makes newcomers feel more at home. Establish a school welcome wagon for your students and parents. After the school year moves past the end of September, whenever a new student enrolls in school, have a welcome team make a home visit. A team of teachers, another parent, and perhaps a guidance counselor can drop by with the same "We're Glad You Are Here" message and information that other welcome wagons use. Such visits instantly establish positive lines of communication.

When thoughtfully designed, some of these suggestions can be successfully implemented in your school to have a positive impact on this aspect of your parent culture.

Education

This section will focus on opportunities for schools to educate parents, not only on how the school's programs benefit them but also on how they can become more effective parents. Very few parents will respond to school initiatives that insinuate they are poor parents who don't know what they are doing. But parents will respond positively to learning opportunities that provide them with the chance to increase their own knowledge. Schools that reflect negative beliefs regarding their parents' abilities will never be highly efficient in the area of parent involvement. The following suggestions reflect an educational focus:

- ◆ Sponsor a parents' university day, at which parents learn what is being taught, how it is being taught, and how they can help their child become a better reader, speller, or math student.

- ◆ Develop a handbook for volunteers at your school. Provide guidelines and ideas for getting the most out of their time at school. Educate volunteers on the legal responsibilities that go along with working with students. Include a section of do's and don'ts in the handbook. Provide training sessions when appropriate. (A sample is located in Appendix C.)

- ◆ Establish a family resource center in every school where parents can seek help from organizations and agencies. Those staffing the center should know how to obtain legal services, financial and health services, and dental care for families in need. Knowing that many Lions Clubs provide free eyeglasses to students with vision problems can be vital information to parents. The state of Kentucky legislatively mandated the establishment of such centers in all schools not meeting certain standards in the early 1990s. Information on establishing similar centers is readily available through the Kentucky Department of Education at http://www.kde.state.ky.us.

♦ Encourage and solicit parent members for all committees, and encourage their service on any school or community governance board. Train all participants on member expectations and group processes.

♦ Invite your parent organization's board of directors to attend faculty professional development sessions. This enables them to have some knowledge of new programs and teaching methods. While you are at it, invite the school board members who represent your area to attend as well. Allowing them to experience and learn alongside the school's staff will give them a different perspective on which to base future decisions.

♦ Sponsor a "Take the Test" day, at which parents come to school in the evening or on Saturday and work sample questions from your state's accountability test. Secure released items from various disciplines and work with parents to answer the questions.

♦ Have Science Day, Math Day, or Engineering Day, at which departments highlight what they teach and how they teach. Any department or academy can have such a day and provide speakers and demonstrations for students and parents. Involving students in either or both roles will increase parent turnout.

♦ Alert service clubs and churches in the community that your staff members are willing to speak at functions regarding school programs. Ask for volunteers and topics that teachers feel comfortable presenting, then distribute the information. School administrators should be the first names on this list. Educators must be willing to promote the positive aspects of their buildings.

♦ Sponsor a "No TV This Week" program to encourage reading and family time. Provide parents with a list of alternative activities that can keep their child away from the television for a couple of evenings.

♦ As a service to parents, provide information regarding the legal responsibilities of hosting an event in the home for students under the age of 18. Laws vary from state to state, but the possible liabilities involved in cases of underage drinking, sexual harassment, unlawful gatherings, and drug use for parent hosts are enormous. Check out the laws in your state and inform your parent community.

- Some schools provide another service by asking parents to sign a parental pledge regarding parties and gatherings in the home. The school collects the information and then distributes it to all parents for their use. If a student asks to go to a party at a friend's house, the parent can check the list and see whether the hosting family has pledged to supervise the gathering (see Appendix D).

- Ask parents on a regular basis about their needs and their families' needs. Schools that ask such questions will come closer to providing appropriate services than those that don't. A sample survey used by Westport Middle School in Louisville, Kentucky, is provided in Appendix E for use as a starting point. Data from such a survey can be used to establish a family resource center (see Item 3).

- The final suggestion uses the needs established through some type of survey to address parent needs. Establish, advertise, and facilitate parent education workshops in the evenings or on Saturdays that are conducted by local professionals or school staff and discuss the topics that parents view as needs. Schedule the sessions on a regular basis and at specific times. Topics and agendas should reflect the interests of the parents. Follow-up sessions can be planned for any topic, and focus groups can be formed if there is a need. This suggestion differs from others in that it is parent driven and is specifically designed to provide parents with information. Topics might include:
  - Underage drinking
  - Getting into college
  - Sexual harassment or abuse
  - Obesity/anorexia
  - How to talk to my child
  - Setting limits and sticking to them
  - Single parenting
  - Family literacy
  - Learning English

There are more than enough suggestions in this section to keep any school working on better parent relations for a long time. It is said that it is foolish to expect anyone to do better until they know better. Find ways to educate your parents so that they can help you help their children more efficiently.

Invitation

The emphasis of this section is very simple and straightforward—make your school a place where parents (and their children) want to be. Pleasant surroundings, a warm climate, and a sense that something is being accomplished will encourage parents to return again and again. The following ideas may help your school in this area:

- Survey the school's buildings and grounds regularly and remove all physical barriers that hinder parent accessibility. Ramps for wheelchairs, elevators that work, well-lit sidewalks, stairwells and hallways, and ample parking spots all fall into this category.

- Set up a welcome station at the main door, staffed by other parents, that can assist visitors with directions and information. For schools that must have a security checkpoint at the entrance, put the welcome station nearby.

- Make sure that the school staff is taught to greet parents and students warmly and genuinely. Adults who can only ask "What do you want?" "Why are you here?" and "Do you have a hall pass/appointment?" are not an asset to your school. Put somebody at the front desk who is positive, helpful, and knows how to smile.

- If parents cannot or will not come to school, go to them. Schedule school meetings, conferences, or parent gatherings in churches, community centers, meeting halls, or any other facilities that will give you a free or inexpensive place to meet. Have other parents help you advertise such gatherings. Don't be surprised if several parents who have never been in your building show up.

- If possible, provide a quiet waiting room for parents and visitors that is separate from the frantic pace of the main office. Comfortable furniture, flowers, and maybe even a fresh pot of coffee make waiting less stressful for all concerned.

- Regularly schedule "eat and chat" opportunities for small groups of parents (generally five to eight) and their children to meet with school leaders. Titles that have worked in some schools include "Donuts for Dads," "Breakfast with the Boss," "Principal's Lunch Bunch," and "Coffee, Cake, and Conversation." The sessions should be held by invitation or by registration with a limited number of participants, should be free to parents, should not last more than 45 minutes to an hour, and should be informal in nature. Asking random students to invite their parent(s) works well for this activity. If the invited parents don't respond, make phone contact and invite them personally.

◆ Design and plan community service projects that address a common need while providing an opportunity for school staff, students, and parents to work side by side. You can clean up a park, paint a schoolroom or hallway, conduct a voter registration drive, work together on a canned foods drive, host a soup kitchen once a month for the homeless, paint a mural in the cafeteria, or do any one of a hundred other projects. Any project is worthwhile if it allows the school staff to connect with the parent community!

Try one or all of these suggestions to enhance the invitational nature of your school. Doing something ensures that you are at least starting your "cultural revolution." Doing nothing ensures that nothing will ever change. The choice is yours.

4

What Can We Do about Parents Who Are Invisible? Strategies for Monitoring Underinvolved Parents

In order to make significant, positive changes in both the quality and quantity of parent involvement in our schools, educators must take on three tasks that are paramount for success:

1. Educators must identify the people they are trying hardest to reach—their parent group.

2. Educators must make an attempt to understand the reasons why parents choose the behaviors and attitudes they exhibit toward schools.

3. Educators must use this knowledge to implement specific action plans designed to motivate parents to become more active.

The previous chapters have outlined the research surrounding the need for parent involvement. All readers of this book will probably agree that involved parents have a positive impact on student achievement. It goes without saying that both educators and parents understand the importance of working together to meet the needs of all students more efficiently. There is also agreement that as students get older, there is less home–school communication and parent involvement. Furthermore, both groups— parents and educators—express a willingness to help the other accomplish common goals. With all of these givens, why do both groups continually crave a better working relationship?

This chapter will examine some of the perceptions, attitudes, expectations, beliefs, values, and barriers that influence school–parent relationships. It will focus primarily on the invisible or barely known parents that schools so desperately need to reach and involve. These parents do not openly dare the school to teach their child (for many reasons), but their involvement, when achieved, can have a significant impact on their child's progress. Specific ideas and action plans regarding this group's recruitment and service will be discussed.

Who Are These Invisible Parents?

All students, no matter what age or school level, live somewhere, right? In the morning they all come from someplace to school, and after the last bell, they leave school and go to someplace else, right? Furthermore, they all live with somebody, right? A parent, a guardian, a relative, a foster home, or a group home. Don't all students go someplace after school to somebody? Though the accurate answer to these questions is no, not 100 percent of the time, this chapter will deal only with the people whom students consider their caregivers. The circumstances of emancipated minors, married high school students living alone, students incarcerated in youth facilities, and homeless students without an address are beyond the scope of this book. Furthermore, the emphasis will be on parents and caregivers, not on the entire community. Educators realize that only a certain percentage of the adults in any school community actually have students who attend their school. The improvement of community involvement—business partnerships, service organizations, legal assistance, media exposure, and so on—though important to a school system, is a related but different topic that requires a different focus.

When we ask who these barely known, almost invisible parents are, the easy answer is that they are the ones who hardly ever participate in school functions or communicate with school officials. They do not respond to phone calls, letters, or requests for their signature. They do not attend parent organization meetings, student orientations, promotion activities, or extracurricular activities. These adults are not present for student conferences, don't chaperone field trips, don't speak on career day, and don't attend mandated Individual Education Plan meetings. Any or all of these behaviors lead to *invisibility*. Every school has some invisible parents, and some schools have a large number. Government statistics (see http://nces.ed.gov/surveys/ssacs/tables/all_2004_tab_21.asp) reveal that parent involvement decreases

- As students get older and move from elementary school to middle school to high school
- As the size of the school increases
- As the urban nature increases
- As the percentage of minority students enrolled increases
- As the percentage of free or reduced-price lunch students increases
- As the number of teachers who teach a child in a day increases
- As the percentage of transfer students within a year increases

For new educators, the foregoing list may reveal new information, but for most school employees, there is nothing surprising in the statistics. Earlier in this chapter, we said that schools that want to improve parent involvement must identify their target group. Knowing that a certain percentage of parents never come to school or that a percentage of caregivers cannot be reached by phone only identifies the extent of the problem. It does not identify who the invisible parents are. Minimum identification includes a name, an address, the relationship to the student, and any possible phone number. Schools generally maintain a student information sheet on every child and work diligently to keep the information current. Yearly updates in schools that have three or more of the factors listed previously may not be enough. Schools with all of the factors and large numbers of students will cringe at the enormity of the task, but it is important to make a continuous effort to keep information current. Just as you can only eat an elephant one bite at a time, you cannot reach 2,000 parents until you have reached the first one. The following suggestions may help:

- Distribute a new information sheet every year to every student. All new students registering at any time during the year should also receive a sheet.
- Print the sheet on two- or three-copy NCR paper so that teachers can retain a copy.
- Print the sheet on bright neon-colored paper. When a child comes home the first week of school with a stack of papers to sign, all the white pages look the same.

- Make the return of the form a requirement, and remind students that everyone is expected to return one.

- Do not make failure to turn in a form a punishable or disciplinary issue. This only encourages the students to fill it out themselves with false or uncertain information. After a given amount of time, just give the student a second sheet and ask for compliance.

- Be relentless in the pursuit of this important information. It doesn't matter that it is the second week of October. Your persistence indicates that the information is important and that 100 percent participation is expected.

- Make these information sheets and updates the responsibility of every adult in the building. One secretary working in the guidance office cannot accomplish the task. If the school is organized into small learning communities (grades, teams, departments, or academies), organize in that manner.

- Don't succumb to frustration and conclude that the effort is not worth the reward. The exercise of trying will give hope.

Note: If your current school form needs updating to allow for extra contact information, see that the job gets done. Consider requesting cell phone numbers for all family members, work phone numbers, and both home and business e-mail addresses. Many schools send out their daily bulletins and announcements in electronic form to all their stakeholders by e-mail. If we can send the information to teachers, then with the proper database, we can send it to all students and parents with only two more mouse clicks.

While the gathering of information is the first step toward identifying "invisible parents," follow-up steps are necessary. Checking for missing sheets and outdated information is an important part of the process. Teachers should never stop trying to update student information sheets.

The final step in the identification process is to answer the question, "Which parents haven't we seen, talked to, communicated with, or engaged in school activities?" In many schools, data are kept on the number of parents attending the open house, the number of phone calls successfully completed, or the number of parents returning the surveys. What we don't do regularly is identify who hasn't responded to our school efforts. The parents and caregivers on this list are the invisible ones. It is imperative that this list be created, monitored, and updated regularly. Whenever there is a faculty, department, grade-level, team, or academy meeting, ask as part of the agenda, "Who haven't we made contact with yet?" If each person present takes one name and makes a concerted effort to contact that person before the next meeting, some of the invisible parents will be reached. One parent, one home, and one educator each meeting will reduce your invisibility percentage.

Remember that a school cannot improve parent involvement without knowing who these invisible parents are. Without effort on the part of all school employees, nothing will change. This last list of reminders, though simple and mostly common sense, can have a huge impact on the success of your identification program:

- A fill-in-the-blank information page that has more than a single sheet is less likely to be returned to school.

- Bright-colored paper makes for a higher return rate.

- Make sure the form is available in all the languages spoken in the homes of your students. Parents who cannot read English cannot fill out a form that is written in English.

- Ask for any e-mail address that stands a chance of being read by a parent, and create a Listserv to send regular communications from the school.

- Set up competitions between grades, departments, homerooms, or academies with prizes for the highest rate of return.

- Assign a specific staff person to oversee the task of identifying invisible parents. This person can coordinate the efforts of the small learning communities.

- Update the "Who haven't we talked to lately?" list on a regular basis. Many schools make an effort to contact parents in August and September, but by the time October rolls around, the energy level is lower and other priorities begin to take over. The most successful schools are those that make invisible parents a priority all year long.

Why Do They Do What They Do?

Once a school has established a database of barely known parents, the next step is to determine, if possible, the reasons they are invisible. Schools lament the fact that the parents they need to talk to the most never call or show up. When our efforts fail to reach the invisible parents, we never progress past our frustration at the lack of response. "We did so much to make this event special and they still didn't come" is often heard. In some schools the targeted efforts end here, and after years of these types of frustration, a general feeling that "Why bother, it won't do any good" develops. Schools must get past this feeling and consider the essential questions: Why don't these parents become involved? What can we do to address those reasons?

The premise of this book is to address the concerns, perceptions, expectations, and realities surrounding parent involvement. The success of our joint efforts toward improvement in this area depends greatly on our ability to understand and appreciate local dynamics. Consider the following scenarios. Pay attention to both what is said and what is implied.

Whenever educators get together, the conversation eventually includes the topic of parent involvement. We discuss the "state" of parenting in today's world. We lament the lack of parent involvement, saying, "Parents today just don't support the schools like they used to," or "When I was I was a kid, my mom was always at school being nosy about things." We yearn for the good old days when parents taught children responsibilities, right from wrong, manners, and so on. We exchange war stories about the worst parents ever. Sometimes we share a success story about how one parent's involvement helped change our school. Eventually, as the conversation starts to burn out, someone will attempt to summarize by stating (always in a convincing, matter-of-fact tone), "You know, I really hate to say it, but parents just don't care anymore." Those assembled nod in tentative agreement and move on to other topics such as teacher pay, the new legislation on core content, or the district's inability to provide enough air conditioning. The gathering ends and the educators go their separate ways, feeling very happy that they had the opportunity to discuss common concerns with their colleagues, but no closer to changing any of their perceptions regarding parents, nor any closer to changing the situations that have led to their conclusions.

On a different evening in a different part of town, or during a coffee break at the job site, or at a church gathering, a different group of adults begin a casual conversation about the issues in their lives. Eventually that conversation turns to how well the community schools are doing and their perceptions about education. The adults will share their war stories about the worst teacher ever, the principal who can't find time to talk, the curriculum that seems watered down, and the safety of their children. You might hear statements like this:

◆ "When I went to school the teachers controlled us pretty well, but they let kids get away with everything nowadays."

- "My teachers used to call my parents every time I did something wrong. I can't remember the last time I heard from one of my kid's teachers."

- "I am sick and tired of hearing all that garbage about self-esteem, and the whole child, I just want them to teach my kids."

- "The teachers always seem to be complaining about everything instead of just doing their jobs."

- "How can a student make it to fifth grade and not be able to read? I just don't understand what's going on up there."

- "Can somebody please tell me what they are spending my tax dollars on?"

There will also be some positive stories shared about a special teacher who changed their child's life or an educator who made a difference to them. These adults almost always agree on how hard it is to be an educator in today's world—perhaps more openly than educators admit how hard it is to be a parent. Somebody will always say, "I couldn't be a teacher. I wouldn't last a week. I would kill some kid, or get fired for telling some smart aleck where to go." Somebody may eventually summarize by stating, "I hate to say this, but it seems like schools don't care as much as they used to." There are some nods of agreement, and the gathering ends. Folks are glad they had a chance to talk, but there has been no agreement on what the schools should do or how to change either their perceptions or the realities.

In both cases, those involved in the discussion speak with passion, conviction, and a sense of urgency for things to get better. They seemingly believe, based on experience, that what is being said represents the way things really are. These beliefs and perceptions cause both groups to behave in the manner and fashion they do, which in some cases only reinforces the negative perceptions of the other group. There may indeed be parents who honestly and genuinely don't care at all about their children, but they are certainly few and far between. In more than 35 years of dealing with parents, the authors can honestly say they have never met a parent who purposely and knowingly set out to damage one of their children. By the same token, we've encountered few educators who cared absolutely nothing for the welfare of children. It has been our experience that neither absolute offered by either group represents how things "really" are.

The question still remains, why are some parents invisible and unknown to school personnel? Their behaviors seem to indicate they don't care, but the reality is either that they have no choice except to be invisible or that they choose to be invisible. The popular author and television psychologist Dr. Phil McGraw often questions troubled guests by asking, "Why do you continue to do things that you know are harmful to yourself and others?" All human beings behave for a reason, either consciously or subconsciously. "What is it you are getting out of this type of behavior?" McGraw's pointed style and commonsense approach could be used by school officials to address the invisible parent issue:

> Why don't you become involved with the school when you know it can only help your child?

or

> What do you gain by not being involved?

or

> What are you getting out of being invisible?

These are the essential questions that must be answered in order for action plans to be effective at meeting the needs of parents. The only way schools can get answers about why parents are invisible is very simple—ask the question. This may appear to be overly simplistic, but common sense says much more than that. Many schools send out parent surveys on a regular basis, asking parents to rate the school on some sort of scale. (If your school does not do this at least once a year, you are missing out on an opportunity to gather important data that will help in making decisions.) The survey asks about aspects of the school program and data are generated, stating, for instance, that 76 percent of parents are satisfied to highly satisfied with the guidance program. While this may be wonderful news, if the return rate is only 55 percent of the parents, the school still does not know why 24 percent of the returnees are unsatisfied with guidance or what the other 45 percent think about the guidance program. Schools have to ask the essential questions. When we look specifically at invisible parents, we usually find the two groups mentioned previously:

- ◆ Those who believe they have no option except to be invisible.
- ◆ Those who choose to be invisible.

When educators ask the "why" question of the first group, they encounter some of these answers:

- ◆ I have no transportation.
- ◆ I am disabled and can't leave the house.
- ◆ I have to stay home and watch the other children.
- ◆ I can't afford a telephone.
- ◆ My child doesn't want me to go to the school.

- I don't speak good enough English.
- I am moving out of town in two weeks, so why bother?
- I work during the day/afternoon/evening.
- My boss will not give me time off.

Every school that reviews this list can probably add three or four more reasons they have heard that fall into this category. The important thing to remember is that the parents using these excuses sincerely believe in most cases that they have no choice except to be invisible. If the school reviews the list and only sees excuses for noninvolvement, then it will only react with disdain. The school's perception of the reasons influences its response and behavior. Successful schools that understand these reasons are genuine and a reality for the parents react differently by initiating programs to overcome these barriers. Look at the list again, and then try these solutions:

- Send a bus to each neighborhood to pick up and drop off parents.
- Have one or two teachers drop by the house for a home visit. Offer to bring pizza or a bucket of chicken.
- During school functions, offer child care managed by older students or other parents.
- Find another parent from the neighborhood or building to drop by and deliver messages from school.
- Find out why the student is reluctant to have his or her parent visit the school.
- Provide translators as needed at school events to overcome the language barrier. Do not forget to provide a person who signs for hearing-impaired parents.
- Offer to assist with the transfer of school records and notifying the new school if possible.
- Adjust the time of parent conference sessions and make them flexible enough to accommodate parents' schedules.
- Offer to call the boss or write a letter to request time off for the parent. Always thank the boss in advance for his or her cooperation.

Each reader of this book has the opportunity to judge how efficient his or her school is at removing these barriers. The school has the responsibility to understand and respond to these concerns on the part of the invisible parents.

Parents who choose to be invisible also need to be asked the same questions. After asking the "why" question of those who choose to be invisible, educators realize that this group's answers are, in many cases, much more difficult to address. This group's responses are often much more personal, more historically motivated, and much deeper than those of the previous group. Consider these comments regularly heard from this group of parents:

- I wasn't very good at school and never graduated myself. I don't see the value in schooling.
- Whenever we do go to school, all we ever hear about is what bad parents we are.
- Last year, the teachers caused our child to hate school, and we can't support them anymore.
- I don't have nice enough clothes for going to school.
- I haven't been to school since the principal at the elementary school did…
- What good will it do? They never listen to us anyway.

Issues such as these, and many others not mentioned, are very difficult to deal with. They are deeply rooted and often have nothing to do with the parents' current situation. Intuitive educators realize that the perceptions and anger expressed in these comments must be addressed by the child's current school and teachers before parents will choose to become involved. Every year, each student's situation encompasses the previous year's perceptions, attitudes, and frustrations. The transition years when students change schools—elementary to middle or junior high or middle school to high school—are particularly important. Schools that understand this process and design programs to establish trust and meaningful relationships with all parents will be more successful at winning over parents who have chosen to be invisible in the past.

In order for the rebuilding of home–school relationships to occur successfully, certain conditions must be present, and schools must exhibit behaviors that encourage these relationships. How educators react to invisible-by-choice parents will determine the ultimate success of any action plan. A positive perception of your school will be enhanced if educators keep the following ideas in mind:

- Be genuine in your desire to include all parents in the learning process. Efforts that are motivated by a desire to win an award for the most parents involved, or that are done merely as a part of a mandated ritual, are totally transparent to parents, who have their warning system on high alert at all times.
- Do not dismiss or embrace the reasons parents give you in response to the "why" questions. If we dismiss parents with statements such as, "Oh that's foolish; I'm sure that they didn't mean that," or "How could you have come up with that?" we are saying that their feelings are foolish. Likewise, a total embrace of the rea-

sons with statements such as, "Yes, I know that is true," "Now that you mention it, we hear that a lot," or "That is a terrible thing to happen" can be damaging to others. The best advice is to acknowledge the feelings as real and then ask for the opportunity to do a better job this year.

Try not to make absolute promises to fix anything. A sincere statement that your school will do everything in its power to see that the situation is not repeated is the best route.

Ask the parents what specifically the school can do for them to overcome the situation that hinders their involvement. Some very simple adjustments on the part of the school can pay huge dividends in this area. Likewise, if something cannot be done to accommodate a parent's needs, it is often better that they know up front that their request cannot be honored.

With purposely disengaged parents, it is helpful if there is one staff member who becomes a conduit for all interactions. Simply state, "Mr. and Mrs. Jones, would it be okay with you if I become your primary school contact from now on? I would like to volunteer to be your go-to person here at school. If you have any questions comments, or needs concerning school, I would be more than happy to look into things for you." The development of a meaningful relationship of a one-to-one nature helps invisible parents overcome some of their misgivings.

It is not impossible to find out what motivates parents to act the way they do; it just takes time. The important fact to remember is that if the school does not ask the "why" question, then it cannot respond as effectively to parent needs. The bottom line is very elementary: Parents who want to come to school and want to be involved do. Parents who don't want to come to school and don't want to become involved don't. Both groups act this way for a reason. Find the reason, and you will involve more parents.

What Can Schools Do That Will Make a Difference?

The final section of this chapter will offer some specific ideas for schools to address these invisible parents. Words such as "perceptions," "attitude," and "relationships" have been mentioned many times in the previous pages. All progressive school leaders understand that these terms, along with many others, blend together to establish the culture of a school. The culture of the school—warm and welcoming or cold and concrete—determines parents' response to all aspects of the school's programs. Schools that want to improve the level and quality of parent participation must change the school's culture from one of…

- We've tried that before and it didn't work.
- We're wasting our time with these parents.
- The reward is not worth the effort.
- Why bother?

...to one of...

- We can't be successful without our parents.
- We will keep trying until we find something that works.
- Our parents do care and are capable of helping us.

In order for change to occur, a school must get serious about its effort to improve and have a plan to make it happen.

Getting Serious

In recent sessions at the conference of the National Middle School Association, at the convention of the Southeast Region Education Board, through the Web site of the National Association of Elementary School Principals, and at several Parent Teacher Organization workshops, participants were asked to gauge how serious they were about parent relationships. Perhaps each reader should also respond to this assessment to determine his or her school's level of commitment.

Planning for Parent Involvement

A school's desire to improve its relationships with parents does not need explanation. What schools want are suggestions. Many schools express concern and lament the lack of parent involvement, yet they have no concrete plan to improve the situation.

Answer "yes" or "no" to the following questions to see how prepared your school is to involve parents:

- Our school has a written, prioritized school improvement plan.
- Our school plan specifically lists improved parent support as one of its top three priorities.
- The need for improved parent support in our school was identified by analysis of some type of data over a two- or three-year period.
- The school plan has a quantifiable goal written as part of the parent support item. For example, "Contact 100 parents" or "Increase the number of parent conferences by 5 percent."

- Parent involvement has a specific action plan that states what will be done and how this activity will affect the current situation.
- The action plan identifies several educators by name, not an anonymous committee, who are responsible for implementing and monitoring the action plan.
- The action plan includes a concrete budget to be used solely for the purpose of enhancing parent involvement. The budget specifically states how much money will be allocated, where the money will come from, and who will have the authority to spend it.
- The action plan has an evaluation component that requires regular reports and summaries to be shared with all stakeholders.

After honestly answering the above items, educators can easily see how much emphasis has genuinely been given to this issue at their school. If a school really wants to make significant changes in any aspect of its culture or climate, it must have a plan that is consistently talked about, acted on, and monitored.

After judging their previous efforts to address parent involvement, many schools find they thought that they were serious regarding this issue, but their actions rarely progressed beyond the first three or four items on the list. It is suggested that all schools, through a committee or as a faculty, review their efforts from the last five years using the instrument, then make plans for the coming school year to include all eight qualifying conditions. Remember you are changing the school's culture, and taking the task seriously is the initial step. Good luck.

Suggestions for Addressing Invisible Parents

The following suggestions have come out of discussions with educators across the country over the last 20 years. They are offered as ideas to address the three steps listed at the beginning of this chapter: (1) Who are the invisible parents? (2) What are their reasons for noninvolvement? (3) What actions can the school take that will help change their receptiveness toward becoming involved? A very important cautionary note is needed before proceeding. Just because this chapter has identified invisible parents as a target group does not mean these ideas should be limited to that group. What works for those parents we consider our toughest challenges also works for the willing parent—in some cases more so than what we are currently doing.

School Walk-About

With all due respect to Crocodile Dundee, a school walk-about can pay huge dividends. Load a bus and travel to or just walk to a neighborhood that your school serves. Have groups of five to eight school staff members take address cards and knock on doors. The only agenda is to make contact, introduce yourselves, check contact information, and personally invite whoever answers the door to come to the school for orientation or open house. Take the opportunity to distribute school contact information. This is not a formal meeting but an introduction. The perception that "These teachers took the time to come down here" can overcome historical beliefs that the school does not care. Knock on all the doors where your students live during your first trip. This gives the message that you are targeting all parents, not just those who are hard to reach.

Ride the Bus/Car Caravan

In rural communities or in school districts that cover large areas and are served by many schools buses, get on the bus and ride around. This works with both morning and afternoon routes and is highly successful when the school and home are separated by several miles. Make arrangements to have two or three staff members get on the bus with the students. Whenever the bus stops, the teachers get off and interact with any adult who is dropping off or picking up students at the bus stop. The agenda is the same as the walk-about: meet and greet, personal contact, and an invitation to become a partner with the school. In addition to meeting parents, the teachers will get a firsthand idea about where and how the students live. The car caravan works in much the same way, as parents are often around whenever a bus stops. Two or three teachers in their cars follow each bus or selected buses. When the bus loads or unloads students, one teacher gets out of his or her car and chats with these parents. The bus continues to the next stop, where the second teacher does the same thing with the same agenda. The third stop is for the third teacher. By the time the bus reaches the next stop, the first teacher has finished talking and has caught up with the caravan and repeats the process.

Faculty Phone Blitz

At one of the year's first faculty get-togethers or meetings, sit down as a group and call parents. Almost every educator has a cell phone, so the idea is not hard to implement. The act of having the whole staff in the same room, engaged in the same activity creates a feeling of camaraderie among the staff. Staff members who are reluctant to call on their own will participate because this is a whole staff event. The school may choose to operate from a list of invisible parents previously identified by the small learning community or the guidance office. When done at the beginning of the year, the school might choose to give a script to all the staff so that all parents receive the same message. Something very simple often works best:

> Good afternoon, my name is _____, and I am one of the teachers at (student's name) school. All the teachers are calling parents right now to introduce ourselves and tell you how excited we are about the upcoming school year…(invitation to open house, check on parent contact information, tell the parents how to contact school).

Making the effort and talking to an adult is probably more important than what is said. Limit the activity to 45–60 minutes every time it is done. The phone blitz can be repeated at the beginning of each grading period or semester. After the initial effort, target homes and parents that have not been contacted—the invisible ones.

Building, Street, Block, or Neighborhood Partners

Identify one or two parents who are actively involved with the school from a specific building, street, or block where there are invisible parents. Ask them to help. These parents can knock on doors, call their neighbors, or drop by for a visit. The agenda is always the same: Make contact and urge involvement. When a school walk-about is not an option, the parents could go with one or two teachers and introduce them to their neighbors. Parents in small groups can conduct their own walk-about without a staff member; this action is less effective than when a school employee is part of the group, but it will still produce results. Whenever a school can enlist the support of those who are positive about its programs and policies, it strengthens the school culture. When these people share that enthusiasm, every stakeholder will benefit.

Family School Picture Day

The yearly taking of school pictures for records, yearbooks, and fund-raising is an activity that occurs in almost every school in America. There is always a day or two set aside, notifications to parents to encourage full participation are sent out, and some kind of schedule is set up that tells which pictures will be taken, when, and where. With this activity, invite all parents to come to school and have their family portrait taken by a professional photographer. For many parents, no matter what level of involvement they have, this might constitute their best and only opportunity to have an affordable picture made. As a hook to get parents to come to school, this activity works wonders. Inform parents of the tentative schedule and have the photographer take both school shots and family pictures. This is a win–win situation, with the only drawback being time. The parents come to school. The photographer sells more portraits. The school receives more money, and the invisible literally become visible, at least in a photo.

Perhaps the most important piece of information that needs repeating is that nothing will change in a school unless the staff decides to change it. Begin changing your school's culture today.

5

When Parents Try to Run the School: Program Activities for Balancing Overinvolved Parents

In a book that is focused on the importance of parent involvement and how schools can improve their "parent culture," it may seem strange to include this chapter. Some readers may even dismiss the notion that there are actually schools where overinvolved parents create a problem. In reality, however, these schools do exist, and parents who want to "run the show" do create problems in some districts. In almost every parent involvement workshop, there will always be at least one educator who asks, "What suggestions do you have for schools that have too much parent involvement?"

Twenty years ago, this situation may have been almost unheard of, but as parents progress from being baby boomers to Gen-Xers to Millennials, the evidence of their increased involvement is becoming more significant.

There has always existed a small percentage of parents who regularly collide with public schools over philosophy, budget, curriculum, and governance. Parents who are upset with a teacher over a grade, a coach over playing time, a band director over music selection, or a principal over disciplinary actions have been a part of public schools for years. Their actions, though unpleasant and hard to deal with, have not, for the most part, prevented schools from the task of educating tomorrow's leaders. "Helicopter parents" (always hovering over their children) and "smother mothers," though annoying at times, have not caused schools to withdraw from their belief in the research that overwhelmingly shows parent involvement to be a cornerstone of academic success (Strauss, 2005). Currently, however, in the age of No Child Left Behind, high-stakes accountability, and more stakeholder empowerment, the patterns clearly indicate that the percentage of dissatisfied parents is increasing and that the uneasiness between parents and schools is also increasing. Faced at times with unrealistic parent expectations, growing demands on educators to never make a mistake with any student, and a willingness by some parents to hire a lawyer at the first sign of a conflict, schools have begun to feel the impact of these negative relationships. Overinvolved and overbearing parents have even been identified as a major contributor to the alarming number of young teachers who quit during their first three to five years on the job. A 2004 Met Life survey of teachers in America reported that 73 percent of new teachers said many parents treat them as the enemy and not as partners. In all, 31 percent cited talking to and involving parents in the life of the school was the biggest challenge they faced. In the past, when a student got into trouble at school, he or she also got into trouble at home. Now it seems that getting into trouble means calling your parents on your cell phone as you walk to see the principal, telling them your version of the persecution. Then your parents meet you in the office, ready to defend you against all foes. How has the common goal of the school, teachers, and parents working together deteriorated to this point?

In this chapter, we will look at two aspects of the overinvolved and overbearing parent issue. We will attempt to answer some of the "why" questions surrounding this growing trend and try to offer some concrete strategies for dealing with this growing phenomenon.

This chapter covers three topics:

1. Understanding the current conditions
2. Commonsense suggestions for all educators
3. Specific strategies that teachers and administrators can use to address the problem

These sections, though not addressing every situation at every school, when studied and implemented, can help lessen the negative impact of this segment of a school's "parent culture."

Understanding the Current Conditions

There are surely countless examples of how parent behaviors have interfered with school goals, and every school has at least one war story to tell regarding overbearing parents. The following examples help illustrate the point that tensions between schools and parents are on the rise:

- The parent who congratulated his son for "getting in the last licks" when he attacked another student in the principal's office following a confrontation with the other boy in the hallway. The parent's response to the additional five days of suspension was to state to the boy, "I don't care about the suspension, we will just go camping this week instead of school."

- The parent who, during a conference about his son's grades, couldn't understand what the big issue was and asked, "Why do you think math is so important? I get along fine without it."

- The parents who sued a school that attempted to suspend their child for cheating, blaming the teacher, who had "left the tests out on the desk and made them too easy to steal."

- The father of a young student who loudly cursed the teacher on bus duty when he was asked to move his car from a no-parking zone while the child watched and listened.

- The teacher who told a student she must work harder on her reading, only to have the little girl's angry mother complain that the teacher had "emotionally upset her child."

- The parent who, when asked by the health teacher to conduct a family fire drill at home to practice safety measures taught in class, responded with a scathing letter stating, "My wife and I many years ago left the formal education system and will no longer do homework assignments."

There cannot be many valid reasons for these types of confrontations, but their occurrence in schools around the country is receiving more headlines every day. The parents involved may offer explanations for their behavior, but these do not help educators make sense of the phenomenon.

In a May 5, 2007, article in *Time* magazine titled "Parents Behaving Badly" (Williams, 2007), the author offers several insights into the problem. His thoughts include the following:

- Many parents are confronted with a fast-paced world that is less forgiving and much more complicated, and therefore they believe that perfection from grade school through graduate school is the only road to success for their child.

- Some parents see student failures as being caused by others, as the failure cannot be their child's fault or their own. Therefore, they look to place the blame elsewhere, and many times it lands on the educators.

- Parents now believe more than ever that societal status is connected more firmly to the exceptional, selective, world-class school that their child attends than it is to the type of car one drives or the neighborhood one lives in.

- People who wouldn't dare tell others how to do their jobs find it totally acceptable to tell teachers what to do. And parents such as these seem to demand meeting times with the teacher that are convenient for their own schedules rather than the schedule of the school or the teacher. Often, parents accuse the school or the teacher when a problem exists rather than accept that their child could be at fault.

These insights all seem to share a the common thread that today's parents seem to question not only the teacher and the school but authority in general. They also question how governments are managed and where their tax dollars go, demanding answers in all arenas of their lives. The level of autonomy once enjoyed by many professions simply is not tolerated by today's parents.

Kathy Checkley (2000) shared the ideas of principal Marianne Young of Monument Mountain Regional High School in Great Barrington, Massachusetts, in an article for the Association for Supervision and Curriculum Development's *Education Update*. According to Young, when facing less than positive news about their child, parents often think about unrealized expectations for their child rather than the actual issues raised by the school. Young states, "If Sally has trouble reading, we as educators make those phone calls we see as productive and positive. Let's call right away. Let's get remedial help. We're going to help Sally. The parent may have a different reaction. The parent may only hear that his child has a flaw, that something is not right. They hear that Sally is not going to sail through school and life without any problems. The parent then must let go of conscious or unconscious dreams he had for that child—and he may resent our call." Young draws a parallel between bad news from school and the stages of the grieving process. The hope, surprise, denial, and finally acceptance regarding news from school can be easily identified in the behavior of overbearing parents. The following information will allow the parallels to be more clearly established:

Parent–School Relationships and the Grieving Process

According to Young (cited by Checkley, 2000), this cycle starts at the beginning of school and continues throughout the year.

Phase 1—Hope: It's a new beginning. Everyone cooperates.

Phase 2—Disappointment: This comes with the first telephone call bearing bad news.

Phase 3—Fear: The parents' initial reaction is to question the news.

Phase 4—Avoidance: Then denial, blame and evasion set in.

Phase 5—Restoration: Finally, parents become willing to listen and accept help from the school and teacher. The result is a positive relationship and mutual appreciation.

In addition, Young believes that schools benefit when leaders strive to understand how parents feel and to validate their emotions. A parent who feels that he or she can walk into school and be heard by the administration and by the teachers will leave that school and say, "They listened to me."

When parents don't feel that their voices are heard, they will exercise their power whenever and wherever they can. It can result in voting down the budget or letters to the editor. Young's ideas have a great deal of merit and shed valuable light on the phenomenon of too much parent involvement. When schools pay attention to the needs of parents, both spoken and unspoken, the likelihood of "open warfare" is diminished. Any attempt on the part of schools to welcome parents as active partners in the education process will always pay dividends within the "parent culture" of the building.

Commonsense Suggestions for All Educators

Every time parents come to school, they have an objective in mind. Whenever they enter our school building they are on a mission.

They need to

- ◆ Drop off lunch money
- ◆ Pick up their child
- ◆ Bring in a class project
- ◆ Make an appointment
- ◆ Attend a conference

- Check on their child
- Get something fixed

Successful schools realize that these "missions" happen every day and prepare for their constant occurrence in various ways. The previous chapters have suggested ways to involve more parents, strengthen home–school communications, and avoid common mistakes in the arena of parent involvement. This section will focus on more strategies that have been proven over time to work with overinvolved and overbearing parents.

Whether parents come to school already angry, prepared to get angry, or asking questions so that they won't become angry, they all have two things in common:

1. They come out of love, care, and concern for their child.

2. They come reflecting their interpretation of a parent's role.

Every educator, even those who have been abused by some parent in the past, must appreciate the fact that parents who stick up for their children are more valuable than those who give up on them.

At times, we may not admire the manner in which they approach us, but we must acknowledge the situation they are bringing to our attention. The first suggestion, then, is to make every attempt to separate the parent from the problem. When angry parents begin to question your sanity, credibility, judgment, and credentials, try to focus on the issue at hand. Use paraphrasing, active listening, and professional restraint and avoid becoming defensive and angry. When you become defensive, parents know it, and the chances of working together as partners toward a win–win situation diminish. The "feel, felt, found" strategy (see Chapter 3) will help address these circumstances.

A second suggestion along these lines is to remember that there are a great number of statements that should never be made to parents when they come to school. Professionals know that these statements only escalate the tensions and emotions inherent in every situation. The following five examples should go at the top of the list of statements you should never make to parents:

- "We have done all we can do to help Andrea with this problem. It is now up to you and her to correct the situation." This defeatist message says that the school has given up on the child. Parents with limited parenting skills have no place to turn at this point for help and may become even more demanding.

- "Your requests are completely unreasonable and totally out of the question." This statement sends the message that the speaker has already passed judgment on the request and dismissed the issue.

Because the statement personalizes the request by using the pronoun "your," the parent will not focus on the fact that the speaker has denied the request but instead will take it as a personal affront.

- "If (the problem) is not corrected immediately we will be forced to (action)." There are two messages in this statement that parents will object to. The first is that they have little or no time to work with their child regarding the problem. Very few school problems develop overnight, so to believe they can be fixed "immediately" is a fallacy. The second is the threat of failure to make corrections. No parent will respond positively to a threat.

- "Now I understand why Samuel behaves/performs the way he does." This statement, when said with disdain, may be true in some instances, but it is a direct attack on the way the parents have raised their child. Furthermore, it implies that every problem a student has is caused by faulty parenting. The focus becomes a personal insult instead of a focus on the child. Always focus on listening and finding a solution to the problem, not establishing blame.

- "The only answer that the school is comfortable with is (solution)" or "The only thing we can do under policy is to (solution)." Both statements convey the message that the school will look no further for options. The parent has just heard that further discussion is pointless. Much like the first example, defeatism is very clear, and the reaction of parents to this "my way or the highway" message will almost always be negative.

The purpose of listing these examples is to illustrate how communication is essential in all aspects of dealing with overbearing or overinvolved parents. Unfortunately, these and other examples are many times a part of the Individualized Education Program (IEP) for students with special needs. This process, which is inherently filled with passions, emotions, and the potential for severe confrontation, does not need more fuel in the form of these types of statements to burn out of control. Nicholas Martin, in his book *A Guide to Collaboration for IEP Teams* (2005), powerfully suggests that all school personal be trained in how to communicate and collaborate effectively with parents. He offers over 100 solutions for parent complaints most often heard stemming from IEP meetings. The ideas and suggestions that Martin shares, though specifically directed toward the IEP process, apply to all parent encounters.

Other commonsense suggestions that warrant review by all staff include the following:

- Always remain calm and speak in a quiet voice.
- Avoid criticizing, lecturing, preaching, and threatening.
- Stay focused on the issues, not the person.
- Avoid profanity and objectionable language.
- Never resort to name calling (direct or implied).
- Don't speak in educational jargon and acronyms.
- Give an opinion as your viewpoint only—a possible solution rather than a mandate.
- Allow parents time to speak and don't interrupt.
- Practice active listening.
- Don't assume the parents understand what has been said. Always check for clarity by asking for feedback. For example, ask, "What is your understanding of what has been said?" or "Can I clarify any of our discussion for you?"
- Avoid general descriptors and make clear statements regarding performance and behaviors. Instead of saying, "He has a bad attitude," "He is irresponsible," or "She is lazy," describe the student's actions and behaviors: "She has failed to turn in the following assignments..." or "He has been tardy to class (number) of times." These specific descriptions are much clearer to parents.
- Get parents' names and roles correct. Use last names and correct courtesy titles (Mr., Mrs., Ms., Miss, Dr.).
- Be aware of your body language and hand gestures. Do not encroach on parents' personal space.

Williams (2004) suggests that almost all first-year teachers lack many of these commonsense strategies and therefore find themselves overwhelmed by pressures from parents. Because many new teachers only have the experiences they remember from their own childhoods and their own parents' interactions with educators, they face parent confrontations virtually helplessly. Devastation and defensiveness are the result. Williams recommends that pre-service teachers be exposed to these realities and be taught, perhaps through role-playing exercises, the skills necessary to manage overinvolved and overbearing parents.

In an essay titled "Dealing with Overbearing Parents," Kellie Hayden (2007) offers more commonsense suggestions to try when a "helicopter parent" lands in your classroom. She suggests the following:

- Find time to allow parents an opportunity to express all of their concerns and issues during a parent–teacher conference.

- Make sure all major assignments come with a detailed project sheet and specific instructions (a follow up call to ask "Did you receive _____" might enhance this strategy).

- Allow parents to organize the field trips, be responsible for the class newsletters, or solicit other volunteers for the school social so that they will remain busy in a productive way.

- Volunteer to send home weekly grade sheets on student progress, and take every opportunity to write a quick, positive note in the student's agenda book. This strategy is very proactive on the teachers' part.

- Discuss serious situations with the school principal so that he or she can put forth an extra effort to make the parents feel comfortable and to reassure the parents about the safety of the school and the quality of education their student is receiving.

Hayden's suggestions apply to just about every parent encounter. Though specifically shared to address overbearing parents, her common-sense suggestions are valuable when facing any angry or unreasonable adult. Readers are encouraged to add these ideas to their professional toolboxes.

In many cases, overinvolved parents will request or demand conferences in order to fix a problem, get to the bottom of a problem, set the record straight, or to tell us what to do. Whether the parent is angry over a problem or just insistent on talking, the best response is to set up a meeting. A set time is always preferable to a "drop-in" demand to talk to you on the spot. An article from the *Virginia Journal of Education*, "How to Have More Successful Parent Conferences" (1984), reviews many of the commonsense ideas already shared, while adding the following suggestions for improving efficiency in dealing with parents face to face:

- Make the first call of the year, before the parents call the school, if you anticipate problems based on past history. A positive call at the beginning of the year can lesson or "head off" difficulties later.

- Invite all parents and stakeholders to the meeting so that all involved receive firsthand information.

- Have your paper work done. Have examples of the student's work available. Have test data handy. Be ready for questions. Structure the session with a flexible agenda.

- Double-check with the parents on the issue(s) to be discussed, and avoid becoming drawn into issues you are not prepared to discuss.

- Stress collaboration and focus on strengths as well as weaknesses.

- Ask for parents' opinions. Focus on win–win solutions. Be prepared to offer possible solutions, and to listen to theirs.

- Try to wind up on a positive note and summarize what was said. Leave with a written action plan signed by the attendees, and keep a written record of the meeting.

- Allow enough time for everyone to talk, try not to rush, and be willing to meet again if needed. (p. 18–20)

  (Used with permission of the Virginia Education Association)

The ability to remember and use these suggestions on a continual basis in all situations can ultimately mean the difference between success and failure with overinvolved parents. The most important concept to keep in mind is that the home and the school are partners in the education process.

Always look for solutions that benefit the student. Reminding all participants that the only purpose for having the meeting is to help the student will reinforce the importance of working together.

Though it is very important with overinvolved parents to know what to do in many different situations, it is equally important to have an idea of what *not* to do. Veteran teachers from New York were asked for their thoughts regarding common mistakes that teachers, particularly young teachers, make when dealing with parents. The article, "Ten Things You Should Never Do in a Parent-Teacher Conference" (1998), suggests the following:

- Don't summon parents to the classroom and direct them to sit in front of your desk. They may be anxious or fearful. Greet them warmly and sit together comfortably around a table.

- Don't begin by focusing on the student's problems. The student is their beloved child, and parents want us to recognize their concern. Start with the student's strengths before raising problems if possible.

- Don't dress too casually. You are a professional, and professional attire communicates that message. Do dress in a manner that reflects the meeting's importance and your respect for the parents and the student.

- Don't wing it. Rehearse what you want to say. Practice introductions, prepare an outline, and have a checklist of topics.

- Don't rely on verbal descriptions of behavior and work. Avoid subjective statements. Do show examples of a students' work and demonstrate how the parents can help the student improve.

- Don't point, blame, or become aggressive. Do use positive body language, listening skills, and maintain eye contact.

- Don't dominate the meeting or share everything that might be a problem. Do think hard about how much information is necessary or can be handled at one time. Allow time for parents to express the concerns or questions they may have. Engage them in planning the best ways for both parties to help the student.

- Don't send the parents home empty-handed. Offer curriculum handouts, classroom rules, parenting materials (see Appendices F, G, and H) or other materials that they can review at home. Make sure that any planned actions are written down and that parents receive a copy.

- If you must use buzzwords, get in the habit of using parenthetical statements. For example, "This year we will use math manipulatives, which are objects, like maybe a set of marbles, that let kids touch and experience what is meant by mathematical symbols, in our math class."

- Don't end the meeting on a negative note by recounting the student's problems. Do end positively by setting goals and outlining how parents can help implement the action plan. Schedule future meetings if necessary. As a final thought, send a follow-up note to say, "Thank you for coming to school and working with us," to the parents within two days of the meeting.

(Used with permission of New York State United Teachers)

It is hoped that the commonsense suggestions contained in this section have provided a firm foundation that will improve the reader's efficiency when dealing with almost any type of parent.

Remembering that, in many cases, it is not what you say but how you say it, will lead to more healthy parent interactions while at the same time creating a more positive parent culture.

Specific Suggestions That Teachers and Administrators Can Use to Address the Problem

The suggestions in this final section are included primarily for educators who believe that their overinvolved and overbearing parents are different from those found at other schools. Even though administrators may firmly believe that the situation at their school is unique, in reality, there is a very slim chance that is true. Whether with great success, or with dismal failure, somebody else has dealt with a similar problem. The following ideas are offered as possible solutions to situational problems. The previous section offered suggestions of a general nature that could be applied to many situations, whereas the suggestions here are more specific and should be considered more carefully as they apply to each school's situation.

Case Study #1

The parent is a certified "smother mother" who has continually disrupted the education of her three daughters at the elementary school. She does so by making surprise classroom visits, demanding that the teachers implement various modifications for her daughters, none of whom has been identified as having special needs, and by constantly alerting the local media to "widespread" injustices at the school. She has been banned from coming to school without an appointment by the elementary school principal. Her oldest child will be starting middle school in the fall, and the mother calls during the summer to schedule an appointment with the middle school principal. As the principal of the middle school—fully aware of this parent's history—how would you respond?

Case Study #2

An hour ago, you informed the star basketball player that he is ineligible for the playoffs because of academic difficulties, and now the student and a very vocal parent are sitting in your office. The player is silent while the parent speaks:

Principal _____, I am appealing to your common sense, because I know you have more than the teachers have. My child is a good kid who doesn't cause you any problems at all. He has never been sent to the office for discipline. He tries hard, but his teachers won't help him. Basketball is all he has, and I won't allow you to destroy his dreams. I know he is a little slow, but we both know that the team can't win without him. You have to let him play! If you go through with this, I know it will be because you never give poor kids a break. I don't care what you have to do, but he'd better play tomorrow. I am bringing him to the game with me, and he will be dressed, and I will see that he gets on the court! My lawyer and every television station in the town will be with us.

Do you have any suggestions for this principal?

Case Study #3

As principal, you have arranged a conference with a parent to discuss why Advance Placement calculus will not be offered next year at the high school. The parents arrived at the office, along with two other sets of parents whom they invited. After finding enough chairs for everyone, the seven of you sit down in your office. The last parent to enter closes the door. The parents are articulate with their questions, but they seem to ignore your explanation that you cannot staff a full position for fewer than 10 students and that if you did so, the other classes would be overcrowded. Everyone enters the discussion at this point, and the 6:1 odds are very unfavorable. The parents do not raise their voices, call you names, or become angry—they just continue explaining that their children, "who are the leaders of next year's senior class," deserve the opportunity to have AP calculus taught, no matter what the consequences. One parent reminds you that he knows members of the school board, while another flatly states that she is not leaving until you agree to have the class taught. "We don't want to have to send our kids to parochial school, but we will if we have to," states the third parent. The meeting continues with no resolution. Does this class get offered next fall?

We will come back to these case studies and their resolutions at the end of the chapter. Undoubtedly, many of you have already identified the primary barriers within each case by focusing on the described behavior and language of the parents. Possibly, some readers have already decided what their response would be if they were the principal. We hope that the following suggestions will allow readers to formulate more than one option for each case.

Ask For More Time

In many situations in which an immediate resolution is not needed, it is better to ask for more time rather than make a mistake in how you answer. Additional time allows you to reflect privately on the demands, formulate other options, ask others for advice, and separate the problem from the parent. Extra time allows you to collect additional information from the teachers and guidance counselors. By listening intently to the parent and showing concern regarding the issue, you can be accommodating and avoid an immediate disaster. When you do ask for time to think about a request, always state when you will get back to the parent with a response, and always meet that deadline.

What Is It That You Want?

Many overinvolved or overbearing parents do a wonderful job of explaining what they *don't* want, but they have never really considered what they *do* want. Sometimes acknowledging to a parent that you understand their concern or their request and then asking them what he or she would like you to do about it can help prevent a crisis. If the response is "just fix it!" be prepared to ask how. Asking for parents' suggestions makes them partners in the solution. If you cannot grant a request because of school policy or legal concerns, then say so, but ask for other options in the same breath. "I'm sorry I can't do _____ because of _____, but I am willing to try something else if you have another suggestion." This statement stands a better chance of being accepted by a parent than, "The answer is no and that's final."

Protect The New Teachers

We discussed earlier how some parents are unwilling to make allowances for inexperience and are much more confrontational with new staff members than with seasoned veterans. As a faculty, discuss the situation as it applies to your school and set up policies that assist young teachers in dealing with this type of parent. Here are some ideas that have been tried successfully in schools:

- ◆ Establish a comprehensive mentoring program that pairs each new teacher with a veteran teacher for the first year.
- ◆ Initiate a school policy prohibiting a staff member from meeting with a parent alone (add a guidance counselor, team teacher, or administrator).
- ◆ Take down the directory in the front hall that lists the teachers' names and room numbers so that an angry parent must either ask for directions or wander the halls looking for the correct room if he or she wants to confront a staff member.
- ◆ Set up interdisciplinary teams and academies that meet with parents as a group.
- ◆ Practice telephone conversations using a school template, and role-play actual scenes from past parent confrontations.

Be the Professional

In any parent meeting, these words are very valuable and always make perfect sense. In our public schools, we must remember that they apply to our own professionalism. If you lose your temper with a parent, you have lost the battle. If you yell back at somebody who is shouting at you, there is no hope of compromise. Don't be affected by threats that are directed at you, and don't direct them at a parent. Don't allow yourself to be intimidated, and do not intimidate a parent. Cursing back at a person who is cursing at you might make you feel better, but it solves nothing. Some educators question the fairness of turning the other cheek, but the only hope for sanity in a confrontational situation is a professional demeanor.

Know Your Own Limits

The best time to seriously consider what you will tolerate from any adult or parent is before a conflict occurs. All of us have different points at which "enough is enough." We strongly suggest that you know your own limits before you are pushed to enforce them. Whether you consider such limits rules to live by, personal standards, or codes of conduct, they must be preestablished and practiced constantly. Allowing one parent 30 minutes to rant and rave while allowing a different parent only 10 minutes creates questions of favoritism and preferential treatment that cloud future issues. It is acceptable to state expectations regarding time limits, behaviors, and language at the start of any meeting. In some cases, it helps establish a more professional atmosphere. The second part of this suggestion is to have a clear idea of what your response will be when a parent goes beyond your personal limits. Educators who have considered what they will do and say when a situation turns ugly stand a better chance of remaining professional. Practice statements such as, "If your profanity continues, I will have to end this conference," "I am concerned when you shake your fist and yell at me," "Please stop immediately, I cannot deal effectively with your concern when I am worried about your threats," and "I appreciate your passion for your child, but personally calling me names and insulting my family will not help the situation."

Take It Higher

When a conference or conflict has reached an impasse, this strategy is sometimes the only solution that will allow the meeting to end. The parent wants you to do something, and you have refused several times, but seemingly he or she will not take no for an answer. When faced with a deteriorating situation such as this, try a statement such as, "I don't believe that we can reach a common solution at this point. I have given you my decision, and without further information I cannot change my position. I would encourage you to contact my supervisor and ask him/her to review my decision if you would like. If they instruct me to consider another solution, I will follow their instructions. His/her name is _____ and can be reached at (phone number)."

This type of statement reinforces the strategy of asking for more time. Always write the supervisor's name and phone number on a card and hand it to the parent. Immediately after the parent leaves your office, inform your supervisor that the parent is headed their way, the decision that you made, and why you acted as you did. Sometimes overbearing or overinvolved parents will respond more openly and calmly to a central office person than one at the building level. Do not overuse this strategy by referring every minor incident to a higher authority. This creates a "sky is falling" environment, and your parent community will begin bypassing your office and start going directly to the top with their problems. If your decision is overturned, you have still done what you thought was right in the situation. Don't whine or complain if this happens—you suggested the alternative.

Keep Your Friends Close and Your Enemies Closer

When parents demand involvement, it may be to an administrator's benefit to structure that involvement on his or her own terms rather than the parents'. Involve this type of parent whenever possible. Seek out the parent's advice on upcoming school issues: "I just wanted to run this by you. What do you think?" Invite the parent to serve on a school committee or participate in the parent council or parent organization board. Surrounding a negative influence with many positive ones always lessens the impact. If you have the time, attend the meetings the parent becomes a part of so that you can stay abreast of his or her actions. Inviting this parent to make a presentation on career day can result in an eye-opening experience for him or her. Some schools have also adopted this "enemies closer" philosophy by asking parents to serve at the school welcome center, organize community service projects, or assist in the media center.

Find The Time Now

When an overinvolved parent pops in for "just a minute," many educators know that 10 minutes today may save them two hours tomorrow. How a principal handles drop-ins sends a very clear signal to the parent community. If the principal responds by saying, "I don't have time right now," "I can't talk to you today," or "I am busy right now," without any qualifiers, the parent almost always becomes an adversary. If possible, find the time right then, or within 15 minutes, to talk to the parent. ("Just let me finish doing _____, and I will be right with you."). If you are too busy, always qualify your response with an alternative suggestion. When you ask questions such as, "Can I call you in about an hour?" "Are you able to come back after lunch?" or "What does your schedule look like around 2:30?" the message the parent hears is much more positive. If you have another scheduled appointment, explain the time constraints by stating, "I can only give you about_____ minutes right now because of_____. We may not be able to reach a solution right now, but I will at least have an opportunity to listen. How does that sound?" These suggestions mesh very easily with the first strategy (asking for more time) and help buy time without seeming annoyed or disinterested.

An Ounce of Prevention Is Worth a Pound of Cure

There is legal precedence in our country that if no policy is established and practiced before an incident occurs, then any actions taken by the organization after the incident are subject to critical review and may be found arbitrary. Educators who are aware of this find it much easier to be proactive in the establishment of guidelines for dealing with overinvolved parents than to be reactive. Schools that collaboratively develop and implement clear guidelines and expectations for student, staff, and parent behavior do so in an effort to minimize misunderstandings. Though it may be impossible to write a policy for every situation, when a policy exists and is followed, it gives educators more solid ground to stand on when dealing with parents. The examples that follow come from schools across the country. They have all been specifically developed to help educators bring more consistency to their actions and address situations that have occurred in the past. As you review the list, if a suggestion addresses an issue at your school, consider writing a corresponding policy. Does your school have a policy that

- Outlines how staffing is done and how many students must sign up for a class in order for it to be included in the master schedule?

- Establishes rules and expectations for school volunteers? (see Appendix C)

- States how fund-raising money will be used, who can authorize its spending, what types of fund-raising are acceptable, and how often these projects may occur?

- Describes expected chaperone behavior on a field trip?

- Tells parents the guidelines for gifts that are given to school and states who will control the use of such material items? For example, a parent donates $5,000 worth of equipment for the weight room but only wants the football team to use it. How about the parent who buys four LCD projectors for the school and insists that they are only for the science department's use?

- Defines the school's response to a student with AIDS, a gun in the building, a teacher who uses profanity, or a student who is drunk at the senior prom?

- Explains the guidelines for flower or balloon bouquets sent to school in celebration of a student's birthday?

- Ensures equal educational access to all extracurricular activities (field trips, band camp, cheerleading uniforms, prom tickets) regardless of the financial situation of the family?

This list could include hundreds of examples; however, the point is not to identify every possible situation a school could face, the point is to encourage schools to review their existing policies. If a situation has caused conflicts in the past at your school, adopt a policy to address any future occurrences. Implementation of these suggestions and those contained elsewhere in this chapter will help any school deal more successfully with overinvolved parents.

All three of the case studies presented in this chapter had the potential to become explosive situations, yet all three were ultimately resolved positively through the use of specific strategies and common sense. Some readers may even have peeked ahead in the chapter to see how these scenarios concluded. If you did so, or if you wanted the resolution of the case studies, please understand that the intent was to have readers formulate the endings, review the suggestions, and then determine whether their own responses would be the same after doing so. The three case studies were all true cases, and the following explanations for each are the actual resolutions.

Solution to Case Study #1

The principal set up an appointment with the parent in July, when he had less stress and more time. He asked questions about the girl's background and accomplishments and sent a clear message to the parent that this would be a new year at a new school for her oldest. He asked the mother what she would she like him to do to address her concerns; he gave her his cell phone number and permission to call him any evening at home between 6:30 p.m. and 8:30 p.m. (set limits). He asked her to serve on the school climate committee as a parent member and encouraged her to become involved with the PTA. He also inquired about her biggest concerns with the elementary school, and, while not acknowledging the validity of everything she said, he did assure her that the middle school had different policies. Finally, he asked for her cooperation, requesting that she never go directly to a teacher's classroom without an appointment or without receiving permission from him personally. The "smother mother," though she continued to be overinvolved to a degree, became a recognized parent leader at the school. She served three terms as PTA president, filled two terms on the site-based management council, and spent countless hours tutoring students during her five-year association with the middle school.

Solution to Case Study #2

The principal demonstrated restraint and professionalism during the conference and did not step on the verbal land mines the parent had laid in her path ("You have more common sense... The teachers won't help him... You don't give poor kids a break... My lawyer and the television team will be here tomorrow"). She acknowledged the parent's concerns and ended the conversation by stating that she would review the school's and district's policies and contact the father in the morning. She immediately went to the two teachers' classrooms in which the student was failing and collected records and information regarding his progress. She then went to the coach to get his input on the situation. She called the district athletic director and reviewed the athletic guidelines with him. She also inquired about his availability the afternoon of the next day. She contacted the parent that night (meeting a deadline early sends the message that you are indeed working toward a resolution) and set up a conference for 1:00 p.m. the next day. She informed the parent that she, along with the athletic director, the coach, the teachers, and the guidance counselor, would be meeting with him and his son. She invited him to bring his lawyer if he thought it was necessary. This shocked the father but sent the message that the principal would not be threatened with legal action. At the meeting, the athletic director explained the policy and again stated that the boy was ineligible. The coach explained that if the student was allowed to play that the entire team would be sanctioned by the state athletic organization. The teachers described the reasons for the failing grades, and the student was asked to verify the statements, which he did. The teachers also expressed a willingness to help in any way they could. The group brainstormed alternative solutions and reached consensus on the following:

- The boy did not play that night.
- He attended Saturday school to catch up on missed work that weekend.
- The student would spend his lunchtime with the teachers until he achieved passing grades.
- He would receive extra help after school from the teachers. This would cause him to miss only the first half of practice.
- He would play next week if all conditions were met.

The student followed through with the plan. The team won without him that night; his grades improved; and he played in the next three games, leading the school to the regional finals. Neither the lawyer nor the television crew ever came to school.

The principal in this case asked the parents for their suggestions on how he might go about meeting both his staffing needs and their requests. He realized that if the school had had a policy on staffing, his position would have been much stronger. The parents offered no solution to the situation, nor did they seem inclined to seek one. He ended the meeting by stating that he would continue to explore alternatives and told them all that they would know the status of the course by the end of the current school year.

The principal consulted with the trigonometry teacher to get information about the students and was told there were three additional students who could benefit from having AP calculus whose parents were not so vocal. Even with six students, offering the class would still cause overcrowding in the other math classes. It was the guidance counselor who suggested scheduling a "zero hour" before school on the master schedule. The principal approached the math teachers and asked for a volunteer to teach an early morning class before first period for those six students. The principal, under contract, could neither mandate nor pay any volunteer, but he did promise to waive the usual required bus duty, lunch duty, game duty, and committee membership duties for any volunteer.

A teacher who always came to school early jumped at the offer, as she had a small child and would save money on after-school care if she could leave school at 3:05 p.m. Additionally, she would get an opportunity to teach the brightest students in the school. The principal invited the six students and their parents to a conference before school ended and explained his suggestion.. Even with the requirement that transportation was to be the responsibility of the parents because buses did not run that early, all the parents agreed enthusiastically. The principal's actions turned adversaries into allies.

Conclusion

The reality of public education today, combined with parents' desire to ensure the best for their children, almost guarantees that overinvolved parents will continue to exist. The thoughts and ideas shared in this chapter cannot make these situations and conflicts disappear entirely. The hope is that the suggestions will prompt educators to think and act in a manner that encourages compromise and deescalation while at the same time minimizing the impact of this segment of the school's parent culture.

6

Special Challenges: Assisting Parents and Students in Urgent Situations

An essential component of a curriculum for parent involvement is a set of clear guidelines for dealing with parents and students who are in crisis. There are many types of urgent situations that students and parents might experience. The first is when the student has a personal crisis that requires intervention from adults. Another is when the student is a part of a school that is experiencing a crisis. Other situations come from outside sources such as weather or transportation incidents. One parent's or student's perspective of an emergency or a crisis may not be the same as the person from whom they are seeking help. As in all helping relationships, listening is the key to helping parents and students through trauma and crisis. The following are several common crises that might occur during the school year. Several suggestions are offered for meeting the special challenges, but these suggestions are not intended to be the only ways in which these challenges can be met. If a school has identified the parents in their school and knows what their needs and expectations are, this entire process will be easier in a crisis.

Special Challenge #1:
The Student Who Is Failing

One of the most common crises that require urgent intervention from adults is the student who is failing one or more subjects. The less parents know about the impending failure, the more of a crisis it becomes for them. Those who have been aware all along have probably been working with the teacher and have already tried several ways to solve the problem. When parents are called or receive a failing progress report, they may feel helpless to do anything to help their child. They may be receiving mixed messages from the student and the school. They may see their student complete work at home and not realize that most of the work is still in the book bag or locker and has not been handed in to the teacher. Typically, the failure has to do with late or incomplete work. A conversation between the parent and the student will involve the student's admission that he or she does not have the work completed and cannot do it at home because he or she did not bring the textbook home. At that point, the parent feels powerless to help the student without the proper materials. The student is off the hook for doing the work because the book isn't available.

Meeting the Challenge

- Homework hotlines are helpful, but they work only if the student brings the homework home. If the school places one book from every class in the reserve section of the public library, then books are accessible after school and during the evening. Parents who are serious about helping their child will see that he or she gets to the library to use the materials.

- Be sure that parents understand exactly what their student's options are: What exactly is due, and when is it due? Explain to parents what a rubric is and how it will be used to evaluate the student's work. Give parents a copy of the rubric and the teacher's e-mail address or school telephone number so that they can keep in touch.

- Arrange a three-way conference with the student, parent(s), and teacher that is facilitated by a counselor or administrator. If the parents are upset with the student or the teacher, the facilitator can keep the conversation focused on how to help the student succeed.

  Many schools have grade-level teaching teams that meet with the parents of students who are having difficulty. Be sure that the parents do not feel as if they are outnumbered in the meeting.

Hesitant parents will not return to a school if they feel that the staff is ganging up on them. If one or two team members collect data from each team member, they can share that with the parent in a less threatening conversation.

◆ Ask parents to sign progress reports that are sent home and return them to the teacher. If teachers do not receive signatures, they can be sure that the parents have not seen the progress report. Of course, some students have been known to forge a parent's signature—that can be avoided if the parent is asked to call the teacher to make an appointment for a conference.

◆ Suggest to parents that they set a schedule for supervised, uninterrupted homework at home until the student is no longer failing. Too often, parents will tell a student to do his or her work but don't check to make sure the student is doing just the homework and nothing else. They may have to take away the cell phone, iPod, and television until the work is complete and they have checked it. Teach parents to check the homework by looking at the assignment and the completed work. Some parents use an equivalent minute strategy that involves the right to use the cell phone or television or video game for the same amount of minutes that the student spends on school work. If a student does extra reading, he or she receives extra minutes.

◆ As the school year begins, ask parents to complete an information sheet outlining their hopes for their student. Ask them to list their child's strengths, favorite classes, and outside interests. Ask them how they feel they can best help their student this coming year. Many teachers ask parents to write letters about their child, but for parents with language difficulties, a fill-in-the-blank form is less threatening and more apt to be completed. A sample student information sheet follows.

Student information Sheet

Dear Parent,

The staff at our school is very interested in helping your child succeed. We would like you to fill out this information sheet, which will be given to your child's homeroom or advisory teacher. The more information that you can give us about your child, his or her strengths and needs, and any concerns that you may have, the better we can plan the appropriate learning environment for each student. Thank you for your help. Please call or e-mail us if you have any questions about this form.

Name of student _____

Name of homeroom or advisory teacher _____

Please identify your child's (adolescent's) areas of strength:

Please identify any concerns you have about your child or adolescent in school:

Please describe your child's (adolescent's) learning patterns and organizational skills:

In your opinion, what type of approach to instruction helps your child (adolescent) learn best?

Please describe your child's (adolescent's) interests, hobbies, skills, which may not always be evident in the classroom environment:

Please tell us any family or personal information that you feel will help us teach your child (adolescent):

What goals do you have for your child (adolescent) this year?

Modified from a form designed by Bergmann and Lake Bluff Middle School, Lake Bluff, Illinois.

Each school can add its own questions or revise those that exist in order to meet the needs of their own parent population. One school had a nearby university translate this information sheet into six languages so that parents could respond. They learned that it was worth the time it took to do the translating.

Special Challenge #2:
The Student Who Is Being Bullied or Threatened

Every student has been or knows someone who has been bullied at school. It starts in the early grades at recess and escalates to both subtle and dangerous types of behavior.

In addition to bullying, students are threatened by rival gangs, for being new in the building, and for not fitting in. Today, bullying has spread to the Internet and cell phone voice mail. Parents are often the last to know that their child is being bullied and the impact that bullying is having on their existence and achievement in school.

Children and young adolescents may be afraid to tell their parents for fear of retaliation that is worse than the bullying. Adolescents most likely will not tell their parents but will gather a group of peers for support. They will try to solve the problem on their own and usually create a bigger situation. When their parents finally find out, the student may be depressed, suicidal, or seeking revenge on the bully. Though movies make light of bullies, it is no laughing matter to a student who is being bullied and his or her parents. Parents feel very vulnerable when they fear for the safety of their child in school. For every student who is bullied, there is another student doing the bullying whose parents must be informed. No one wants to hear that their child is hurting others. They may wonder where the behavior is coming from and ask for assistance, or they may totally deny that their child could be a bully and ask for proof.

Meeting the Challenge

- ◆ Conferences with the parents of both the bullied student and the bully must include the counselor or social worker and the student. Depending on the severity of the situation, the counselor can decide whether to meet with the parents of both students together. The focus of the conference should be on solving the problem that these two students do not get along. If a school has not set disciplinary guidelines for bullying, a task force that includes parents, students, and counselors should be formed to write school policy and to establish an education program for students and parents. Counselors should teach students and their parents how to de-escalate a situation by using active listening and "I" messages. Using an "I" message, the speaker identifies his or her feelings about a problem instead of attacking the other person. This makes the listener more willing to try to solve the problem. This process also works when parents are talking to their child or adolescent.

◆ The school can adopt a program such as "Don't Laugh at Me," a project of Operation Respect (http://www.dontlaugh.org). This program can be downloaded at no cost and is designed to create a school environment that is free from bullying and put-downs. While it is available for kindergarten through eighth grade, much success has been found later at the high school level when the program is taught to elementary and middle school students. One key element to this program is a song titled "Don't Laugh at Me."

At a recent parent education program at which the Don't Laugh Program was introduced to parents and students and the song was played, a father asked the school principal whether the school could implement the singing of this song on a weekly basis. He said, "It seems to me that if a school can have a fight song, they can certainly sing a song that develops compassion in kids."

For high school students, a new assembly program titled "Rachel's Challenge" has been designed by a parent, the father of Rachel Scott, the first student killed at Columbine High School. This program is designed to help students reach out to other students who are handicapped, new at school, or being picked on by others. The program provides much information for students and parents about issues related to bullying and threats.

Other programs that help students and parents in threatening situations are available from national organizations such as the National Association of Secondary School Principals (http://www.nassp.org), the National Middle School Association (http://www.nmsa.org), and the National Association of School Psychologists (http://www. nasponline.org).

◆ If a student is continually threatened both in and out of school, parents should seek help from their local law enforcement officers, who will work with the school to try to stop the threats.

Special Challenge #3:
The Student Who Has a Physical Problem

Communications with parents of students who have physical problems require that the school have knowledge of a wide variety of community resources. Physical crises may include drug and alcohol abuse, serious illness, pregnancy, or physical handicap. Each crisis is unique to the individual, but there are resources available for help.

Meeting the Challenge

♦ Make sure that the school has accurate information about the physical condition. Ask parents what information may be shared with teachers and what information is to be kept private. Be sure that teachers know that the student may have to leave school for doctors' appointments or therapy. Introduce parents to the school social workers and counselors who will be the liaisons between the student and his or her teachers. Offer parents information on how to help their student keep up while at home. Determine the student's goals and the parents' goals for the student. Give the parents a consistent contact to speak with at the school.

♦ Offer parent education workshops on dealing with the tough issues that face teens. Accurate information on drugs and alcohol can help parents cope with their use and abuse outside school. Assisting parents in the formation of a parent network for support and social event monitoring is also an effective part of any parent education program. Other parent education workshops should be offered both at the school and online for safety issues related to the school, the neighborhood, and the Internet. These workshops can be offered in conjunction with local social agencies and law enforcement. One school teamed with a local college, law enforcement, and area hospital to offer parents a workshop called "Sex, Drugs, and Rock and Roll." Parent turnout and feedback were excellent, and the session was repeated the following year.

♦ Some schools offer entire programs of study for parents who need to take the GED or gather enough credits to complete their high school education. If the parents are taking classes, their student is more apt to stay in school and out of trouble. Other communities offer special schools for students who are pregnant. These schools offer medical services as well as an academic curriculum.

Special Challenge #4:
The Student Who Is a Part of a Crisis in the School

Every school faces a crisis sooner or later. Some are whole-school crises that are weather related, whereas others are the crises of an individual students that may affect the entire school. Some face crises on a daily basis, others only once in a while. When students are in a crisis situation, the parents must know what the crisis is, what the crisis intervention plan is, and what their role is.

Just as schools have successfully implemented parent involvement plans, they must make crisis intervention a part of that plan. When disaster is imminent or a crisis is taking place, everyone in the school should know his or her role. Many states require tornado drills, fire drills, and lock-down rehearsals. Others have emergency plans that are given to schools for hurricane evacuation and blizzards. Too often, it is the parents of the students in the school who are not sure what their role is or whom to contact.

Technology has changed the way in which we solve crisis situations in schools. The use of cell phones today can both help and hinder the process of solving a crisis. Case in point: A student who was in the high school office to get a late pass overheard the secretary taking a message for the principal, who was in a meeting with parents. The message was that schools should be let out immediately so that students could arrive home before an approaching blizzard. The student called home on a cell phone and asked her parents to come and pick her up. She told other students in the hall, and before the principal could call the bus garage or tell the teachers, parents were calling the school office and arriving to pick up their students.

Life-Changing Events
That Can Create Crisis for Adolescents

There are long-term crises that brew in the school social setting and short-term emergencies that occur on a regular basis when schools are dealing with young adolescents and adolescents. The definition of an emergency or a crisis is quite different for students than for adults. A student may tell a teacher that she has to go to the office for an emergency. The emergency is that she forgot her math paper, lunch, or cheerleading uniform and needs to call a parent to bring it to school. Adolescents have a difficult time sorting degrees of crisis because many of them haven't experienced true crisis in their lives.

There are life-changing events that can create daily crises for students, staff, and administrators. These events happen to many students. Many students cope with the changes and do not need intervention, whereas others can become so preoccupied with the event that they feel frightened and out of control. Some may respond with reckless and dangerous behavior that affects their peers and the school setting.

The following events may or may not need crisis intervention depending on the degree of the crisis, the student's ability to cope, and the support system that is in place:

- Change in peer group or friends
- Change in living arrangements: moving to a new neighborhood, school, or family
- Change in family structure: separation, divorce, or death of parent or sibling
- Change in role models
- Change in academic expectations (transitions from elementary to middle school and from middle to high school)
- Change in parent expectations and involvement
- Change in physical health

Though most of these changes involve the student's family, sometimes the parents are the last to know when a student has changed role models, joined a gang, or is not acclimating to a new environment. Schools may be the last to know when parents have divorced, left town, or are terminally ill. If parents and teachers do not communicate, a small crisis for a student can quickly escalate into academic failure or a larger crisis.

Meeting the Challenges of Crisis Intervention

Step 1: Parent Education

The first step in crisis intervention for parents is education about the developmental characteristics of young adolescents and adolescents. Parents today are not sure what is normal behavior, what their adolescent is involved in (both in and out of school), and how to handle typical adolescent outbursts, moodiness, and withdrawal. They want to know not only how their adolescent is doing academically but socially and emotionally as well. They need to know where their adolescent is getting support, who their friends are, and how they cope with stress. They need skills for coping with a crisis situation in the home as well as at school.

Many middle schools offer parent nights that discuss the characteristics of young adolescents, transition to the middle school, and where to go for help as a parent. Though a few high schools offer parent education programs, they tend to focus more on how to get into college and how to improve grades. Parents need to understand how important their involvement with their child is throughout the K–12 process.

The school can tap into existing programs for parent education that are specific to its own population. One such program, The Parent Institute for Quality Education is an organization dedicated to informing and motivating low-income parents to learn how to navigate the school system and find opportunities available for their children. This institute has successfully reduced dropout rates and increased college participation among Latino youth living in California (Kreider, Caspe, Kennedy, & Weiss, 2007).

Brief Strategic Family Therapy is a family-focused program for children and adolescents who are at risk for behavioral problems. Families are included in the program, which promotes parent leadership, parent involvement, family communication, and culturally sensitive parenting skills. It is a parent education program delivered by a counselor in the community, in the school, in the program office, or in the home. The program has been found to reduce adolescent behavioral problems, substance abuse, and association with antisocial peers (see http://www.brief-strategic-family-therapy.com/bsft) (Kreider et al., 2007). Most school counselors can develop and present an informative workshop on adolescent development for parents and should be encouraged to do so.

Step 2:
Creating a Crisis Intervention Team and Plan

Every school should develop a crisis intervention team that consists of administrators, counselors, teachers, parents, students, community emergency personnel, transportation personnel, school security, office personnel, the school nurse, school security, bilingual resource personnel, and special education personnel. Some schools choose to have two separate committees, one for natural disasters and one for man-made disasters.

The role of each person on the committee should be clearly defined and communicated to the entire school and parent population. Parents from each grade level should be represented on the committee and their roles clearly defined.

The following questions should be resolved by the district administration before the initial meeting of the crisis intervention team.

- ◆ Should the team administrator be the principal or another administrator?
- ◆ What role will students play on the committee and in a crisis?

- What outside resources are familiar with trauma in the school setting? Is there a current list of these resources to distribute to the committee?
- Where will briefings be held during a crisis?
- What role will parents play in a school crisis?

Step 3: Defining the Parent Role

Determining the parent role is crucial to the safety and success of any crisis intervention. Adolescents and young adolescents often do not inform their parents of the policies and practices of the school. Therefore, the school must be sure that all parents are given written policy statements for crisis intervention. Those policies must be clear and offer the following:

- Whom at the school they should call if there is a family emergency
- Whom they should call if the school phones are not working in an emergency
- What the student should do if the school has to close and the parent cannot be reached
- What the transportation policies and routes will be during an evacuation

The information gathered from parents for each child must include the following:

- Where are all the places that a parent can be reached in an emergency?
- Which parent should be called first, second, and so on?
- Are there any special needs of the child, such as handicaps, medications, cue words for calming?
- Where the child should be taken if the parent cannot be reached and the school must be closed?

Parents have enough trauma just dealing with normal development in teenagers, and they have a hard time knowing what is normal behavior and what is a crisis. They may overreact at the wrong time and fail to react at the right time. That is why parents should be given information on how to de-escalate a situation with their child. This information can be presented by the school counselors as part of a parent education program.

Step 4: Training Teachers to Deal with Parents and Students in Crisis

Teachers who understand active listening, funneling, and deescalation can help parents in a crisis situation. Active listening skills are developed with practice and implemented with empathy. Teachers are taught to ACT:

Attend: make contact with the student or parent by voice, note, or eyes.

Calm: Use a soft voice to reassure the student that you will help him or her. Take the student away from the current environment if that is a part of the problem or if others are listening.

Treat: Say, "I sense you are (troubled, angry, upset, ill,). Would you like to tell me or someone else what is troubling you?" or say, "Do you need the assistance of a doctor or nurse?"

After teachers have implemented the ACT process, they can then actively listen to the response of the parents or students by

- Paraphrasing what has been said to be sure they understand the correct message
- Asking what action should be taken immediately
- Answering any questions that they have
- Helping them think of at least one way to solve their immediate need
- Getting them to commit to a positive action
- Taking them to the counselor or social worker for further help if necessary
- Arranging a check-back time to see how they are doing

The method of *funneling* (Suchyna, 1998) has two purposes. First, it is used to obtain detailed information about a crisis situation by asking questions of parents that progress from general to specific. For example, "Tell me your concerns about this situation with your child. What is the most crucial concern for you right now? How is this concern affecting your child? What else can you tell me about this issue or concern?"

Inverted funneling helps when parents cannot or will not speak about the crisis. Questions and discussion go from very specific to general. For example,

"Tell me what happened to your child on the bus. How do you think that this incident is affecting your child? How can we help your child deal with this incident?"

Throughout the funneling process, the teacher should continue to use the ACT process. Results of the conversation should be put in writing, and parents should know what the next step is for the parent, the teacher, and the child.

De-escalation is necessary when a parent is distraught, angry, or violent. If the ACT process does not work, the teacher or administrator should use an "end goal" statement such as, "I believe that our end goal here today is to help you and your child. If you do not feel that we can talk about this right now, let's both take two minutes to organize our thoughts, jot down some ideas, and then discuss what we have written or thought about. The question is how can we best help you and your child?" (If the parent does not have writing ability, ask him or her to choose from a list of words or draw a picture). The teacher or administrator may need to de-escalate by moving the meeting to another location that is quieter. Walking will often calm people down because they begin to focus on finding the destination rather than their anger.

Other strategies for deescalation include the following:

◆ Remain clam and do not show fear or anxiety.

◆ Make statements that are simple and direct.

◆ Do not touch the person. Give him or her lots of room.

◆ Don't take the hostility personally, even if it is aimed at you.

◆ Recognize feelings and try to address them. ("I sense that you are angry, upset, etc.").

◆ Offer a choice between two positive alternatives. For example, "Would you like to continue this conversation in five minutes, or put your concerns in writing and then talk about them?"

◆ Be alert for the possibility of aggression.

◆ Attempt to have the person sit down.

If a parent is violent, do not hold the meeting at that time, but explain calmly to him or her that you will not participate in a conference until both parties are calm and considerate. Remember that it takes a person 30–40 minutes to calm down physiologically.

Leave the room if there are no students present and ask for assistance. If a teacher anticipates that a parent may be very angry or violent, have another adult sit in on the meeting to moderate or take notes. Pay attention to your gut instincts and leave the area if necessary. Those rare instances of violent behavior are what makes the news and have led teachers to fear parent contact in some schools. If teachers have been contacted for a meeting with an irrational parent, the administrator should attempt to meet with the parent first to get his or her perceptions and then meet with both the parents and teacher.

If a parent needs de-escalation because of distress, the teacher can ask the counselor to join the meeting. Nothing works better than old-fashioned compassion for deescalating distress. If a parent has just received news that a child is ill or injured, he or she will need factual information as well as caring and concern from the teachers and the school.

Role-playing can help teachers learn to deal with parents who are in crisis. The following case studies can be given to teachers as role-playing scenarios.

Directions for Role Playing

- Ask one teacher to volunteer to play him or herself and another to play the parents in crisis.
- Give the participants one of the case studies.
- Ask the audience to determine what the teacher did correctly and what other strategies he or she could have used. Check to see whether the teacher used the ACT process, funneling, or deescalation.
- Have the "parents" tell how they felt during the role play.
- Brainstorm strategies specific to your student population that may be necessary.

Role Play #1

A high school student has been in a car accident and will be out of school for at least six weeks. Some of her injuries are major and will require much therapy. The parents of this honor student have asked for a meeting with the biology teacher because she is most worried about missing the labs and not getting a scholarship. The parents are distressed not only about their daughter's injuries but also about what she may lose as a result of missing school. As the meeting begins, the mother dissolves into tears and sobs uncontrollably.

Role Play #2

The parents of a student who was injured in a physical education class during an altercation with another student storm unannounced into the teacher's office right after school. The father is extremely angry and has been drinking. The parents believe that the teacher was negligent in maintaining a safe environment and have only heard their child's side of the story. They immediately ask the teacher to resign or they will sue the school.

Role Play #3

The parents of a student who is failing three subjects have asked to see the teachers who are failing their "perfect" adolescent. They assume that it is all the fault of the teachers and have come to the meeting very defensive and upset. They feel that their adolescent is gifted and has never been challenged. Therefore, their adolescent is bored in class and does not really need to do the repetitive work. The student has not handed in any assignments but has managed to pass three tests in each class.

Role Play #4

Parents of two students who have been homeschooled for the first eight years of their education have asked to see the ninth-grade teachers. They feel they have done an excellent job preparing their students for high school, but placement tests show that the students are not reading at grade level and have poor computational skills. In addition, the two students are having trouble adjusting socially to the school. They want their students to participate in athletics and dramatics.

Meeting the Challenge

The more that teachers are aware of the strategies for conferencing with a parent in crisis, the more apt they are to have a conference that helps the student. Because crises cannot be anticipated, all personnel in the school should have information about what to do in a specific crisis. Parents should be given a card that has emergency numbers at the school. The card (placed on a refrigerator magnet if possible) should outline the basic steps to take in case of a school emergency. Parents should have input into the design of this card. It may need to be translated into a second language in some communities. The key is to communicate with parents before a crisis occurs so that students, parents, and teachers will not suffer the trauma that can occur after a major disaster. Students, parents, and teachers all have their own definitions of crisis and emergency. Having a plan will help everyone prepare for a time when crisis affects students, their learning, and their parents.

Appendix A

A Plan for Involving Parents

A Plan for Involving Parents

The staff of _____ School will ensure full opportunities for parent participation:

- Resources and forms will be made available in the parents' first language as often as possible.

- School personnel will be available to translate communications to assist non-English-speaking parents.

- During conferences conducted with parents, accommodations will be made for the varied schedules of parents, physical barriers will be removed, and child care will be provided with advance notice and when available.

- Parents will be consulted on an ongoing basis about how the school can work with them for the betterment of their child.

- Opportunities will be provided for training on parenting skills, literacy skills, and how to work more efficiently with their child at home.

- Parents will be involved as part of the governing body of the school.

- Parents will be encouraged both formally and informally to comment on school policies.

- The school will encourage volunteer participation from parents and the community at large.

- Transportation to school functions will be provided whenever possible, and home visits will be made in the case of parents with disabilities.

- The school will coordinate with other community programs to provide services to parents.

- Students will be involved in recruiting parents.

- Parent involvement will be made a schoolwide effort.

- Student work will be distributed for parents' comment and review on a regular basis.

- Opportunities will be provided for parents to communicate with principals and other administrative staff.

- The school will provide parents with links to programs and resources within the community that can offer support services to them.

- The school climate will be open, helpful, friendly, and safe.

Appendix B

Parent Participation Opportunities

Parent Participation Opportunities

I intend to support the efforts of _____ School this year. I will...

_____ Attend parent–teacher conferences

_____ Volunteer at school

_____ Attend PTA/PTO/PTSA meetings

_____ Attend Academic Booster Club meetings

_____ Attend site-based council meetings

_____ Run for a site-based council position

_____ Volunteer to be on a school committee

_____ Attend a focus group meeting

_____ Attend the culminating night activities

_____ Attend parent education sessions (e.g.. Portfolio Nights, Reading Night, etc.)

_____ Have a regularly scheduled study time for my child in our home

_____ Have my child rested and ready for school each day

_____ Attend school activities (athletic contests, festivals, open houses, etc.)

_____ Check the homework hotline routinely

_____ Sign each report card and discuss my child's grades with him or her

_____ Call or stop by school routinely to check on my child

_____ Read the school handbook with my child and support school policies

_____ Provide reading materials for my children and encourage them to read daily

_____ Other: _____

Student name: _____ Date: _____

Parent signature: _____

Please return this form to _____ by _____.
                           (teacher's name)   (date)

Guidelines for Volunteers: Families and Schools Together: Fayette County Public Schools, Lexington, Kentucky

Guidelines for Volunteers

Supervision of volunteers: School volunteers always work under the direct supervision of the professional staff at each school and only with those teachers who have requested the service of a volunteer. The Fayette Public Schools are responsible for the education, safety, and well-being of each student. For this reason, you can understand why the teacher, principal, or volunteer coordinator may request the reassignment of a volunteer whose actions are not in the best interest of the school or students.

Confidentiality: As you work with the staff and students, information of a confidential nature may be shared with you. The problems, abilities, relationships, and confidences of students, their parents, and the staff should never be discussed with anyone who does not have a professional right to know. Teachers and volunteers are bound by a code of ethics to keep confidential matters within the school. The staff and students need to know they can trust you. Please do not discuss a child's school progress or difficulties with anyone, including his or her parents. This is the teacher's responsibility. Occasionally, a child may confide in you about family matters or personal problems. Keep this confidential, too. If you feel it is vital for the school to have this information in order to help the student, discuss the child's conversation (in private) with the teacher or principal.

Discipline: On occasion, students may have behavior problems while working with volunteers. However, our schools have detailed discipline plans, and the responsibility for discipline rests with the professional staff. Volunteers may not discipline students. Please make the teacher aware of any discipline problem that may arise while you are working with a student.

Dress and behavior: Take your lead from the professional staff and dress appropriately for the job you are doing. It is best to neither overdress or underdress. Casual clothing is fine, but we ask that your attire be neat and conservative. Your appearance should attract no undue attention. Keep in mind that you are in a position to set an example for students. Your speech and behavior should serve as good models for them to follow.

Health: If you are not feeling well, don't try to keep up your volunteer duties in spite of an illness. You'll accomplish more in the long run if you allow yourself time to recuperate. However, do call to let the teachers know you won't be coming at your scheduled time. Schools are particularly concerned about keeping students and staff healthy. This is another reason for staying away from school if you have a contagious illness.

Find out about school rules: Become familiar with the rules and policies of the school where you will work. It is a good idea to read through the school's handbook. Ask your volunteer coordinator to explain the school's policy for using telephones, eating facilities, fire drills, and emergency procedures. Should you ever have the slightest doubt as to the appropriateness of any matter or action, check with your supervising teacher or principal. A copy of the Fayette County Board of Education policies is on file in the school where you volunteer.

Responsibilities of the staff: Volunteers are an important part of the educational team. The suggestions and opinions of volunteers are always welcome. It is the professional staff, however, that is held responsible for decisions that are made regarding the instruction of students and the management of the school. For this reason, volunteers always work under the direct supervision of teachers and administrators.

Let the staff get to know you: Let the staff know what types of jobs you are interested in doing. Be sure they know what your special skills are so they can utilize your talents.

Be prepared to learn: If you've never been a school volunteer before, you'll find that there are many new and exciting things to learn about the job. Please be aware that some staff members have never had an opportunity to work with volunteers before. It may be a learning experience for everyone.

This material was prepared by the staff of Fayette Count Public Schools, 701 East Main Street, Lexington, Kentucky, http://www.fayette.k12.ky.us. The booklet was distributed to all people who volunteered to serve in one of the district schools. Used with permission of the district.

Appendix D
Parental Party Pledge

Parental Party Pledge

I pledge to the parents and staff of _____
School that any social gathering for which I am responsible (in our residence or any designated area) will be alcohol and drug free. I further pledge to be on site at such gatherings and to chaperone any such gathering to the very best of my ability.

Signed _____, Parent of _____,

Address _____, Phone _____

This pledge was distributed to all parents at the beginning of the year. All returned forms were collated and published in the school newsletter. The list was updated with every issue.

_____ School Parental Pledge List

We, the parents listed below, by our signature, pledge to all other parents of our school community that any social gathering we are a part of will be alcohol and drug free. We further pledge to chaperone and supervise any such gatherings to the best of our ability.

Student Name	Parent	Address	Phone #

Appendix E

Jefferson County Public Schools, Westport Middle School Needs Survey

Needs Survey

Westport Middle School is applying for a Youth Services Center Grant. It is very important that we have your input to determine the services to be offered in the center. Please check (X) the areas below in which you, your child, or your family may need assistance.

Thank you very much for taking a few minutes to complete this survey and returning it to school on or before Monday, February 13. Please return the form to your child's homeroom teacher.

Health Services

- ❑ At-school health services
- ❑ Hygiene instruction
- ❑ Exercise
- ❑ Home safety instruction
- ❑ Help to get appointments
- ❑ Transportation to appointments
- ❑ Nutrition information
- ❑ Immunizations
- ❑ School-based examinations
- ❑ Weight control
- ❑ Wellness

Counseling

- ❑ Death in the family
- ❑ Drug/alcohol use/abuse
- ❑ Spouse abuse
- ❑ Child abuse
- ❑ Communication
- ❑ Divorce
- ❑ Behavioral health
- ❑ Family/marital issues
- ❑ Crisis management
- ❑ Anger management
- ❑ Stop smoking

School/Classroom Help

- ❑ Homework help
- ❑ Tutoring
- ❑ Behavioral problems

- ❑ Attendance problems
- ❑ Motivating my child
- ❑ Academic enhancement

Family Support

- ❑ Welfare assistance
- ❑ Agency link-ups
- ❑ Before- or after-school care
- ❑ Day care for young children
- ❑ Housing assistance
- ❑ Heat/utilities help
- ❑ Employment
- ❑ Summer youth employment

Workshop/Skills Training

- ❑ Family health
- ❑ Job readiness (applications, interviewing)
- ❑ GED classes
- ❑ Parenting
- ❑ Reading with kids
- ❑ Volunteer work
- ❑ Parents as leaders
- ❑ PTSA
- ❑ Giving kids responsibility
- ❑ Helping kids make good decisions
- ❑ Dealing with peer pressure
- ❑ Conflict management
- ❑ Test taking
- ❑ Single-parent issues
- ❑ Money management
- ❑ Helping parents deal with sexuality issues

If classes or group activities are offered, check the time most convenient to you:

- ❑ Morning Mornings (9:00 a.m.–12:00 noon)
- ❑ Afternoons (12:00 noon–4:00 p.m.)
- ❑ Evenings (4:00 p.m.–6:00 p.m.)
- ❑ Evenings (other time)
- ❑ Any time

Used with permission of Jefferson County Public Schools.

Appendix F

20 Ways to Improve Your Young Adolescent's Self-Esteem

20 Ways to Improve Your Young Adolescent's Self-Esteem

1. Make time to talk to your child.
2. Provide time to listen and be listened to.
3. Hug and hold often.
4. Spend time with your child daily.
5. Praise often and sincerely.
6. Treat each other with respect.
7. Encourage and support your child's interests.
8. Set a good example by demonstrating values of respect for learning, respect for the rights of others, honesty, and fairness.
9. Organize household schedules and responsibilities so that your young adolescent has at least one "chore."
10. Share your own growing up experiences, failures, and successes.
11. Be consistent and set clear, reasonable limits.
12. Provide privacy for your young adolescent and respect it.
13. Show interest in your young adolescent's friends.
14. Allow your young adolescent to express feelings of anger/hurt in an appropriate way.
15. Talk about successes and joy.
16. Share family history, point out ancestors' successes.
17. Look for something you can share with your child, such as a hobby or a book.
18. Answer your young adolescent's questions honestly and age appropriately.
19. Celebrate regularly.
20. Help your child set goals.

Source: Loucks & Waggoner (1998). Used with permission of the National Middle School Association.

Appendix G

20 Ways Working Parents Can Volunteer

20 Ways Working Parents Can Volunteer

1. Send or solicit resource materials for school when requested.
2. Prepare audio, video, or print materials to enhance lessons
3. Organize details for special events and prepare for events.
4. Make parent calls or community organization calls to solicit resources.
5. Enter data for special programs
6. Prepare materials for displays, bulletin boards, or special projects.
7. Contact businesses for collaborative projects.
8. Be a resource volunteer for homework, assisting students in the evening or on weekends.
9. Serve on committees that meet at night.
10. Prepare fliers for special events or type newsletters at home.
11. Serve as a reader or reviewer for materials to accompany units or special lessons.
12. Provide pick-up services for the library or other community resource.
13. Scout out locations for field trips and provide information about those resources.
14. Serve as a writer, resource, or typist for school newsletters or newspaper articles.
15. Provide technical assistance to teach computer skills to other parents or young adolescents.
16. Build and teach students to construct sets for dramatic presentations.
17. Design possible advertising or promotions for team or school events.
18. After consulting with school leadership, analyze systems to mainstream school processes or maximize resources.
19. Serve as a mentor for at-risk students or students with special aptitudes.
20. Assist with Saturday or holiday work crews to beautify school grounds or improve recreational facilities.

Source: Loucks & Waggoner (1998). Used with permission of the National Middle School Association.

Appendix H

15 Ways To Help Your Young Adolescents Succeed in School

15 Ways to Help Your
Young Adolescents Succeed in School

Communicate better study habits to your child by:

1. Providing a consistent sleep schedule. (Young adolescents need eight or more hours of sleep.)

2. Providing a well-balanced diet.

3. Establishing a schedule that permits ample time to get ready for school and results in a timely arrival at school.

4. Encouraging your child to set aside time for daily homework and reading.

5. Providing a quiet, comfortable place without distractions to study.

6. Encouraging your child to make wise television viewing choices.

7. Asking in a variety of ways about daily homework assignments.

8. Comparing your child's progress to his or her abilities, not to those of siblings or other children.

9. Praising your child when homework or responsibilities are completed.

10. Creating a Homework Survival Kit (assignment notebook, pencil, paper, pencil sharpener, eraser, scissors, dictionary, calculator, ruler, flat surface).

11. Telling your child that you expect him or her to do homework independently, but you are available if help is needed.

12. Providing transportation to the library or other resource areas when assignments require reference materials.

13. Providing a place where completed work may be stored safely (a folder, a shelf, or a drawer).

14. Discussing homework assignments and providing hints when necessary.

15. Becoming actively involved in homework when teachers have requested family–student interaction.

Source: Loucks & Waggoner (1998). Used with permission of the National Middle School Association.

Resources

AARP: http://www.aarp.org. This Web site offers articles and tips for grandparents who are raising their grandchildren.

American Student Achievement Institute: http://asai.indstate.edu/guiding allkids/studentledconferencing.htm. This site provides detailed information on designing and carrying out student-led conferences.

Association for Supervision and Curriculum Development: http://www.ascd.org. Type "parent involvement" in the search box. You will find lots of articles. The November 2000 issue of *Education Update* is titled "Forging School–Home Links," and the April 1996 issue of *Educational Leadership* is titled "Working Constructively with Families."

Brief Strategic Family Therapy: http://brief-strategic-family-therapy.com/bsft. The Family Therapy Institute of Miami provides training leading to certification in the nationally validated, award-winning family therapy model known as Brief Strategic Family Therapy.

Center for Effective Parenting, Jones Center for Families at the University of Arkansas: http://www.parenting-ed.org. This site provides handouts and tips for parents on communicating with schools.

Center for Research on the Education of Students Placed at Risk, Johns Hopkins University: http://www.csos.jhu.edu/crespar.

Center for School, Family, and Community Partnerships, Johns Hopkins University, directed by Joyce Epstein: http://www.csos.jhu.edu/p2000/center.htm

Child Trends: http://www.childtrends.org and http://www.childtrends databank.org. These sites provide information and research for those interested in the welfare of youth and data tracking children's welfare.

Child Welfare Information Gateway: http://www.childwelfare.gov. This site provides access to information and resources to help protect children and strengthen families as a service of the Children's Bureau, Administration for Children and Families, U.S. Department of Health and Human Services.

Classroom Connections: http://www.nmsa.org. A publication put out by the National Middle School Association. Publications can be duplicated. See the information on parent–teacher conferences (1-800-528-NMSA).

Education World: http://www.education-world.com/a_special/parent_involvement.shtml. Although a company site, it offers many short articles. Especially helpful are the links to other useful sites.

Family Involvement Network of Educators: http://www.fine.org. This site was launched in November 2000 by the Harvard Family Research Project to serve as a hub of resources for family engagement in children's education, and to enable colleagues in the field to connect and communicate.

Harvard Family Research Project, Harvard Graduate School of Education: http://www.hfrp.org. Lots of good information on sources, research, and suggestions. Look for "Family Involvement in Middle and High School Students' Education" number 3 in a series, published in spring 2007.

Middleweb: http://www.middleweb.com/mw/resources/ParentConfs.html. Originally designed by the Edna McConnell Clark Foundation, Middleweb is now supported by Steinhouse Publications and solicits practitioner input. This link leads to information about student-led conferences, but there is much information to be shared at this site.

National Association of School Psychologists: http://www.nasponline.org. Valuable information for tackling difficult issues with children, such as violence and illness.

National Coalition for Parent Involvement in Education: http://www.ncpie.org. This is a valuable site for resources for Hispanic and Latino children and their parents. It offers quick updates on new laws that affect parents' rights.

National Middle School Association: http://www.nmsa.org. This organization offers several toolkits, such as "Increasing Student and Parent Involvement through Student-Led Conferences."

National Association of Secondary School Principals: www.nassp.org. This organization offers articles and materials on parent involvement and crisis intervention.

National Network of Partnership Schools: http://www.csos.jhu.edu/p2000/. Established by researchers at Johns Hopkins University, this organization helps schools, districts, and states develop and maintain programs that promote school–family–community partnerships.

National PTA: http://www.pta.org. This site provides a number of documents offering ideas for teachers and schools to encourage and promote parent involvement in education; includes national standards for parent involvement.

Northwest Regional Education Laboratory, School Improvement Research Series: http://www.nwrel.org/scpd/sirs/3/cu6.html and Oregon Parent Information and Resource Center: http://www.nwrel.org/pirc/index.php. These sites provides free publications that are based on good theory and practice

Operation Respect: http://www.dontlaugh.org. A program and site to encourage respect among kids. The site offers information for kids, parents, and educators. A time-tested program with positive results.

Partnership for Family Involvement in Education: http://www.ed.gov/pubs/whoweare/index.html. A national partnership focused on improving parent involvement and children's achievement in school.

Parent Institute for Quality Education: http://www.piqe.org. This is a nonprofit agency geared toward helping low-income and ethnically diverse families work with their children and schools to bolster achievement. It has links to other good sites as well.

ParentNet: http://www.parentinvolvementmatters.org. This is a grassroots organization that supports parent involvement. Although it has a specific program that it advocates, it also supplies practical information and resources.

Project Appleseed: http://www.projectappleseed.org. This nonprofit, national campaign advocates improvement in public schools by increasing parent involvement in U.S. schools. It has links to numerous related and respected sites and provides a checklist to evaluate a school's parent involvement strategies.

Public School Parents Network: http://www.psparents.net. A site designed and maintained by parents of public school children to serve as an information source and reference guide for all parents of school age students.

Rachel's Challenge: http://www.rachelschallenge.com. A nonprofit organization that provides training and assemblies to foster kindness in schools. It resulted from the death of Rachel Scott, who was killed at Columbine High School.

School Crisis Response: http://www.schoolcrisisresponse.com/parentguidelines.pdf. A publication reprinted from "A Practical Guide to Crisis Response in Our School," this provides parents with information about what to expect from their child or adolescent during or following a school crisis. This document may be reproduced for distribution to parents.

Teachers College Record, from the Teachers College at Columbia University: http://www.tcrecord.org. This site houses articles by Jacqueline Eccles, Kathleen Hoover-Dempsey and others on a variety of issues about parent involvement.

U.S. Department of Education, Office of Educational Research and Improvement: http://www.ed.gov/searchResults.jhtml?st=0&colParam=ED&lk=1&qt=parent+involvement. This site provides free research briefs as well as some practical suggestions.

References

Aronson, J. Z. (1996). How schools can recruit hard-to-reach parents. *Educational Leadership, 53*(7), 58–60.

Baenen, J. (1991). *H.E.L.P.: How to enjoy living with a preadolescent.* Westerville, OH: National Middle School Association. [Available in English and Spanish]

Baenen, J. (1992). *More H.E.L.P.: How to enjoy living with a preadolescent.* Westerville, OH: National Middle School Association. [Available in English and Spanish]

Brough, J. A. (1997). Home-school partnerships: A critical link. In J. L. Irvin (Ed.), *What research says to the middle level practitioner* (pp. 265–74). Columbus, OH: National Middle School Association.

Burkhardt, R. (2004). Family contact: Connecting kids and kin through the curriculum. *Middle Ground, 8*(1), 18–21.

Checkley, K. (2000). Parents are people, too: Leading with empathy and compassion. *Education Update 42*(7) n.p.

Child Trends Databank. (2003). Retrieved December 21, 2007, from http://www.childtrends.org.

Chrispeels, J. H. (1991). District leadership in parent involvement. *Phi Delta Kappan, 72*(5), 367–371.

Chrispeels, J. H. (1996). Effective schools and home-school-community partnership roles: A framework for parent involvement. *School Effectiveness and School Improvement, 7*(4), 297–323.

Chrispeels, J. H., & Rivero, E. (2001). Engaging Latino families for student success: How parent education can reshape parents' sense of place in the education of their children. *Peabody Journal of Education, 76*(2), 119–169.

Cotton, K., & Wikelund, K. (1989). *Parent involvement in education.* Close Up No. 6, School Improvement Research Series, Northwest Regional Education Laboratory. Retrieved December 21, 2007, from http://www.nwrel.org/scpd/sirs/3/cu6.html.

Delisio, E. (2003). More principals e-mailing parents. *Education World,* November 11. Retrieved February 19, 2008, from http://www.educationworld.com/a_admin/admin/admin331.shtml.

Epstein, J. L., & Dauber, S. L. (1991). School programs and teacher practices of parent involvement in inner-city elementary and middle schools. *Elementary School Journal, 91*(3), 289–305.

Epstein, J. L., & Herrick, S. C. (1991). *Implementation and effects of summer home learning packets in the middle grades* (Report No. 21). Baltimore: Johns Hopkins University, Center for Research on Effective Schooling of Disadvantaged Students.

Epstein, J. L., et al. (2002). *School, family, and community partnerships: Your handbook for action* (2nd ed.). Thousand Oaks, CA: Corwin Press.

Finn, J. (1998). Parental engagement that makes a difference. *Educational Leadership, 55*(8), 20–24.

Garvin, J. (1987). What do parents expect from middle level schools? *New England Middle School Journal*, Spring, 8–11.

Gibbs, N. (2005, February 15). Parents behaving badly. *Time 165*(7). Retrieved December 21, 2007, from http://www.time.com/time/magazine/article/0,9171,1027485,00.html.

Harvard Family Research Project. (2007). *Family involvement in middle and high school students' education.* Cambridge, MA: Havard Graduate School of Education.

Hayden, K. (2007). *Dealing with overbearing parents: How teachers can cope with helicopter parents and their child.* Retrieved December 21, 2007, from http://educationalissues.suite101.com/article.cfm/helicopter_parents_land.

Henderson, A. T., & Berla, N. (1994). *A new generation of evidence: The family is critical to student achievement.* Washington, DC: National Committee for Citizens in Education.

Krieder, H., Caspe, M., Kennedy, S., & Weiss, H. (2007). *Family involvement in middle and high school students' education.* Cambridge, MA: Harvard Family Research Project.

Loucks, H. E., & Waggoner, J. E. (1998). *Keys to reengaging families in the education of young adolescents.* Westerville, OH: National Middle School Association.

Marshall, M. (2006). Parent involvement and educational outcomes for Latino students. *Review of Policy Research, 23*(5), 1053–1076.

Martin, N. (2005). *A guide to collaboration for IEP teams.* Baltimore: Paul H. Brookes.

Met Life. (2003). *The Met Life survey of the American teacher.* New York: Author. Retrieved December 21, 2007, from http://www.metlife.com.

National Association of School Psychologists. (2002). *Coping with crisis—Helping children with special needs: Tips for school personnel and parents.* Bethesda, MD: Author. Retrieved December 21, 2007, from http://www.nasponline.org/resources/crisis_safety/specpop_ general.aspx.

National PTA. (1998). *National standards for parent/family involvement programs.* Chicago: National PTA.

National PTA. (2004). *National standards for parent/family involvement programs.* Bloomington, IN: Solution Tree.

New York State United Teachers. (1998). Ten things you should never do in a parent–teacher conference. Latham, NY: Author. Retrieved December 21, 2007, from http://www.nysut.org/newyorkteacher/backissues/ 1998-1999).

Olivos, E. M. (2006). *The power of parents: A critical perspective of bicultural parent involvement in public schools.* New York: Peter Lang.

Parents as Partners. (1997). *High strides.* Westerville, OH: National Middle School Association.

Public School Parents Network. Retrieved December 21, 2007, from http:// www.psparents.net.

Purkey, W. W., & Novak, J. (1996). *Inviting school success: A self concept approach to teaching, learning, and democratic Practice*, 3rd ed. Belmont, CA: Wadsworth.

Robinson, V. (1984). How to have more successful parent conferences. *Virginia Journal of Education, 78(1),* 18–20.

Scott Stein, M. R. (1999). *Parent involvement in education: Insights and applications from the research.* Bloomington, IN: Phi Delta Kappa.

Shepard, D. (2004). Planning for parent involvement. *Middle Matters, 13*(1). Retrieved December 21, 2007, from http://www.naesp.org/Content Load.do?contentId=1377.

Springate, K. W., & Stegelin, D. A. (1999). *Building school and community partnerships through parent involvement.* Englewood Cliffs, NJ: Prentice Hall.

Starr, L. (1998). Bring your fathers to school! *Education World,* June 22. Retrieved December 21, 2007, from http://www.educationworld.com/a_ admin/admin/admin072.shtml.

Strauss, W. (2005). Talking about their generations. *School Administrator, 62,* 10–14.

Suchyna, A. (1998). *Communicating effectively with parents.* Pittsford, NY: Totally for Teachers.

U.S. Census Bureau. Retrieved December 21, 2007, from http://factfinder. census.gov.

U.S. Department of Education. (2003). *No Child Left Behind: A parents' guide.* Washington, DC: Author. Retrieved December 21, 2007, from http: www.ed.gov/parents/academic/involve/nclbguide/parents guide.pdf.

U.S. Department of Education, National Center for Education Statistics. *National Household Education Surveys (NHES) 1996 (Parent and Family Involvement in Education Survey) and 1999 (Parent Interview Survey)*. Retrieved December 21, 2007, from http://www.childtrendsdatabank.org/indicators/39ParentalInvolvementinSchools.cfm.

Virginia Education Association. (1984). *27 tips for more successful parent conferences*. Richmond, VA: Author.

Wang, M., Haertel, G., & Walberg, H. (1997). *Fostering educational resilience in inner-city schools*. Publication Series No. 4, Eric Document Reproduction Service No. ED419856. Retrieved December 21, 2007, from http://www.eric.gov.

Whitaker, T. (2001). *Dealing with difficult parents and with parents in difficult situations*. Larchmont, NY: Eye On Education.

Williams, D. (2005, May 9). Parents behaving badly. *Time. Retrieved December 21, 2007, from http://www.time.com/time/magazine/article/0,9171,1059 461,00.html*

Zill, N., & Nord, C. W. (1994). *Running in place: How American families are faring in a changing economy and individualistic society*. Washington, DC: Child Trends. Retrieved December 21, 2007, from www.childtrends.org.

9 7 7 4